CW00500584

PHYSICIAN'S HANDBOOK

Nicola Cantan

NICOLA CANTAN is a piano teacher, blogger and creator of teaching resources. She has been teaching piano to students of all ages since 2005, and currently runs an innovative and inclusive piano studio in Dublin, Ireland.

Nicola loves getting piano students learning through laughter, and exploring the diverse world of music making; through improvisation, composition and games. You can find lots of creative teaching articles and ideas on her site at: www.colourfulkeys.ie/blog.

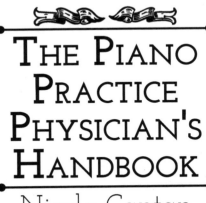

THE PIANO PRACTICE PHYSICIAN'S HANDBOOK

Nicola Cantan

Colourful Keys Books

Copyright © 2017 by Nicola Cantan

All rights reserved. This book or any portion thereof
may not be reproduced or used in any manner whatsoever
without the express written permission of the publisher
except for the use of brief quotations in a book review.

Published in the Republic of Ireland

First Printing, 2017

ISBN 978-1-5272-0700-4

Colourful Keys
78 Durrow road
Dublin, D12 V3A3

www.colourfulkeys.ie

*To my wonderful parents who supported
and encouraged me through years of piano
study, alongside many, many other pursuits.*

*And to all my piano students who make
charming, amiable and enthusiastic
piano practice physician guinea pigs.*

CONTENTS

⟫ Chronic Issues ⟪
AKA Bad Practice Habits

⟫ Fevers & Chills ⟪
AKA Tempo Issues

Contents

⁓ Heart Palpitations ⁓
AKA Beat & Rhythm Inconsistencies

⁓ Vision Impairment ⁓
AKA Symbol & Marking Oversight

⁓ Ear Infections ⁓
AKA Musical Insensitivity

Contents

Your Piano Practice Clinic

What is a piano practice physician?

That's you! Even if you don't know it yet. If you are a piano teacher, you are also a piano practice physician. A piano practice physician is someone who views each piano practice issue through the analytical, problem solving lens of objective scrutiny. In my 12 years teaching piano, I have seen students come up against many pernicious practice maladies, the most common of which are covered in this book. Some of these can have a lasting impact on a student's playing and cause more serious problems down the line. That is why you must be their practice physician.

It's your job to treat your students' piano practice issues as they change, grow and progress through their musical studies. It's your job to diagnose practice issues, find cures, and prescribe solutions for your students. Then it's their job (and sometimes their parents' job) to take action in the six days between lessons.

Let's talk about those six days for a moment. Maybe right now you're thinking: "Yes, but then they don't practice!". This may be true, but perhaps not as true as you think. Chances are you're a wonderful teacher already. I'm sure you give students plenty of advice and instruction on what and how to practice at home only to find they don't practice, or they don't practice enough. And if you're like most teachers you fret, despair and tell them yet again how *important* good practice is.

But how much of your lessons are really spent solving their practice problems? Do you involve them in creating solutions? Do you check up on the practice process and fine tune it the next week? Do you just tell, or do you show, involve and empower your students to practice effectively at home?

If you can train yourself to see each practice issue as

a puzzle to be solved, your students will start to look at their piano studies in a similar way. Diagnostic remedies will not only be a more constructive use of practice time, but your students' minds will be more engaged also. More engagement means their efforts will be even more effective – and they'll have more fun too.

What should piano practice look like?

How often do you find yourself telling your students – or their parents – that they need to practice more? Good practice routines and habits are certainly important; I think we can all agree it's beneficial to discuss habits and expectations for piano studies. What I think is even more important still, and is given little attention, is what practice should look like. If your students think that practice means playing a piece over and over until it's correct, then they are wasting precious time at the piano. If you tell them how to practice at home but fail to implement the strategies in the lesson, then you may be helping them to waste their time. Very few students will follow your instructions once they get home, and there are two main reasons for this.

The first is that verbal or written instructions are not vivid enough, and following these instructions will feel harder than practicing the old way or not practicing at all. The key ingredient in these cures for piano practice ailments is that they make use of your student's imagination. The prescriptions in *The Piano Practice Physician's Handbook* will stick out in a student's mind because they use a range of visual, narrative and gameified techniques that are truly memorable. No one can forget falling in the 'River of Doom' or becoming a 'Bionic Pianist'. Imagination is the most powerful ointment in the piano physician's cabinet, so use it. And, while you're at it, you just might reawaken your own imagination. Grown-ups can learn a thing or two from kids in this regard.

The second half of the magic practice pill lies in the way you administer your cures. We need to coach our students through these processes many times in the lesson before they will follow through at home. Your students may know how they should practice, but that doesn't mean they will take action on their own. This is why the 'In lesson' section of each prescription in this handbook is almost always longer than the 'At home' section. This book is about practice – but most of the work of good piano practice happens in the lesson. The daily time we normally call "piano practice" should be a direct reflection of what happens in the lesson. Good piano teaching means *practicing* practicing during lesson time so that your students know exactly what to do at home.

How to use this handbook

In this book, I will take you through 32 of the most common piano practice ailments and their cures. That much is a given – it's right there on the cover. You will likely recognise some, many, or all of the practice illnesses described in this book from your own teaching. After each description, you will find two possible cures for each of the practice maladies. You can choose the one that best suits the student's age, level and the severity of the condition. For clarity, you will also find a list of the "symptoms" and "related diagnoses". These will guide you in identifying the particular ailment your student is suffering from – and avoiding misdiagnosis – so that you can find the proper cure.

You can read through this book, prescribe the remedies and get some great results from the process. These are practical solutions to problems you will face in your piano studio every day. If you implement them they will work, and you and your students will have more fun and get better results during lessons.

However, I want to encourage you to look a little deeper. Can you take this way of looking at the 32 common piano practice ailments and apply it in all your teaching? Can you stop lamenting the fact that little Johnny didn't get his practice done, and start thinking about how you could better prepare him to practice this week? And how might you be able to solve the underlying problems so that he finds practice easier and more rewarding?

The best way to start shifting your mindset around practicing is to begin implementing the ideas in this book. Read all the way through; jump back and forth to sections that are relevant to you; refer back to it to find a cure for a particular student (preferably before you get to hair-pulling, teeth-grinding stage). Always keep in mind this new way of looking at your role as a piano teacher. As a piano practice physician, each weekly appointment should be a demonstration in the science and art of great piano practice.

A little note on gender

There are many fine piano students who happen to be girls, boys, women and men. However, writing about more than one gender simultaneously is awkward. It's awkward to write and it's even more awkward to read s/he, he/she, or about a fictitious student who changes gender inexplicably from one paragraph to the next. In an effort to not distract you from learning effective practice strategies for your students, I have chosen to give examples using the feminine form only. I hope you will see this as the fair compromise that I do. In my mind, my example student's name is Jane, and she has somehow managed to come up against every single piano practice ailment detailed in this book – the poor darling. So feel sorry for dear Jane, and know that she could just as easily be James or Jeremy.

PART ONE

PART ONE

Chronic Issues
AKA Bad Practice Habits

> *"We are what we repeatedly do. Excellence, then, is not an act, but a habit."*
> **Will Durant**

This first section of *The Piano Practice Physician's Handbook* is one you will refer back to again and again. Some of the CHRONIC ISSUES are completely pervasive, seeping into every piece, scale and étude that your student plays. Others are subtler, or may not be as immediately obvious, but are stealing practice time away from real progress at the piano.

It's difficult enough for today's busy piano students to find the time to practice, so you don't want these chronic practice issues to squander those precious seconds and minutes they've managed to squeeze into their schedules.

As you read through these CHRONIC ISSUES you may find certain students popping into your head. Those mysterious playing habits may begin to become so much clearer. Pay close attention to these ailments and you could save your students countless hours of wasted practice time. And more efficient practice means less frazzled parents, quickly progressing students and greater job satisfaction for you.

1

Start Again Syndrome
Obsessive playing from the beginning no matter the circumstances

This extremely common practice syndrome can lead to many related issues down the road. When students are just beginning their piano studies, starting at the beginning each time they practice a piece will not make a big difference, as most of their pieces will only be a few lines long. As their pieces grow onto a second page and beyond, however, starting at the beginning each time will have a greater and greater detrimental impact on a student's practice.

By playing from the beginning each time, the first few bars get the most practice while the ending gets the least. The student's concentration and mental clarity will also be strongest when they begin playing; students with *start again syndrome* will therefore always be practicing the end of a piece in a less focussed and present way than the beginning.

At its most extreme, *start again syndrome* can mean that if the student makes a mistake in a performance, they will have to go back to the beginning. If the only place they've ever started is the beginning, that's the only place they will be confident starting from, which can be disastrous in a performance situation.

SYMPTOMS

- Insistence on going back to the beginning when one makes a mistake.
- Playing quality that gradually deteriorates throughout the piece.

- Playing that is confident at the beginning but becomes more uncertain as one plays through the piece.

PRESCRIPTIONS

At Sixes and Sevens

In lesson

This is the perfect solution for a piece that a student has been playing for a while already and has developed *start again syndrome* with.

Pick six strong starting points in your student's piece and number them. Roll a die (or use a random number generator) and ask your student to start from that point, and play until the end of the piece. Repeat this process seven times. The randomisation will help her to feel confident starting at different points, and the way it is set up is biased towards the ending, so this section will get the most practice.

At home

Assign your student 'At Sixes and Sevens' practice of her piece for this week. Ask her to put a tick in pencil beside the section number each time she starts from that point. This will not only give her a way to track her progress, but will give you a subtle way to check if she follows through on this practice method at home. Download 'At Sixes and Sevens' tracking charts at: *www.pianophysician.com/bonus*.

Back It Up

In lesson

This method is not for the faint-hearted, but it is the most thorough and reliable cure for students with severe *start again syndrome*. You will need to commit to the process as this solution will need to be administered fully in the lesson and will take a large chunk of lesson time.

Ask your student to play the last bar (measure) of her piece. Once she has played it successfully, she should play the last two bars, then the last three, and so on until she reaches the beginning.

At home

Once you have been through the whole 'Back It Up' practice with your student in the lesson, assign her this practice at home also. Tell her that she is not allowed to start at the beginning until she has backed it up completely, but if she does have less time on certain days she can 'Back It Up' 2-3 bars at a time.

RELATED DIAGNOSES

I-played-it-better-at-home-itis page 21

2

Finger Fascination
The tendency to stare at one's own fingers while playing

This habit can really inhibit students' music reading abilities. When their gaze is permanently fixed on their hands, it is almost impossible for them to read fluently. Students with this issue will often resort to playing by ear or memory to compensate.

Much like a dancer who stares at his feet, this tactic of watching their hands while playing soon becomes counterproductive. When students are looking at their fingers as they play, not only are they not able to read effectively in that moment, but their keyboard awareness will not develop either. As teachers we need to get them over this hurdle and allow them to rely on their sense of touch to navigate the keys.

SYMPTOMS

- Directing one's gaze to the keys more often than to the score.
- Frequently losing one's place in the music.
- An underdeveloped awareness of keyboard geography.

PRESCRIPTIONS

Book Levitation

In lesson

This is probably the most common *finger fascination* remedy and it's popular for good reason. Quite often one session of 'Book Levitation' is enough to cure *finger fascination* for good.

Ask your student to prepare her fingers on the keys, ready to play the piece she is currently working on. Once she is ready to play, hold a book a couple of inches above her hands so she can no longer see them. Then instruct her to begin playing.

It may take a few attempts for her to find her way around the keys, but many students are actually surprised to find that they can do so right away. If this is the case for your student, you may not need any more prescriptions. Her *finger fascination* could have been solved by just this one exercise.

At home

If more intervention is needed, there are a few ways to adapt 'Book Levitation' for home practice. You can directly carry over the exercise to your student's practice by asking a parent to hold the book over her hands at the start of each practice session. You could also fashion a cover out of poster board or stiff card to sit over her hands as shown in the diagram below. I have known teachers to even use basketball dribble glasses (glasses with the bottom half covered over) as a way to tackle *finger fascination* in the practice room.

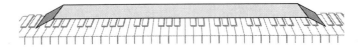

A simpler option is to just leave a note on your student's music that she should imagine the floating book when she is practicing at home. You can then repeat the 'Book Levitation' at each lesson until you feel she has learnt to look only when necessary and not as a force of habit.

Blind Drills

In lesson

This approach takes reading out of the equation completely so that your student can focus entirely on utilising her sense of touch. Ask your student to place her hands in a five finger position such as a pentascale. If your student is more advanced you may choose a full octave scale instead.

Have your student close her eyes or wear a blindfold. Call out notes for her to play, such as "right hand F sharp" or "left hand C chord", as appropriate to her level and current repertoire. Drawing inspiration for these drills from her current pieces is a good way to begin, as she will immediately be able to apply the awareness she is developing in context.

At home

This process should become your student's warm-up for practice in between lessons until the issue is resolved. Instruct her to do the 'Blind Drills' before practicing each piece by placing her hands in the starting position and calling out notes to herself to play. Just by calling the notes out herself she will become more aware of her positioning on the keys – if someone at home is willing to help by calling out the notes at random, that's even better!

Related Diagnoses

Leap Phobia *page 14*
Octave Disorientation *page 17*

3

Leap Phobia
*The habitual slowing of one's tempo
to prepare for a leap*

A common side effect of some piano method books is that students get glued to the keys. In the process of trying to make reading more accessible, many method books leave jumps and changes of position until later. This can create a fear or reluctance with hand leaps across the keyboard.

When students with *leap phobia* attempt these moves they will often be accompanied by an exaggerated ritenuto immediately preceding the movement. The presence of leap apprehension in some students but not others can most of the time be explained by the student's leap technique. Staying too close to the keys and using the wrong focal points are common reasons why these leaps go astray.

SYMPTOMS

- Slowing one's pace prior to a change in position.
- Inaccurate or hesitant leaps across the keys.
- A distaste for pieces with a wide keyboard range.

PRESCRIPTIONS

Bull's Eye

In lesson

This antidote is designed to refine students' focal point technique. Similarly to when kicking a ball, we want our students to look where they're going, not at the hand as it is moving. For some students this comes naturally, but others may need a little nudge.

Place a marker of some kind (counter, sticky tab, eraser) on the key that your student will be leaping to. Make sure she knows which finger is landing on the marked key. Ask her to practice the leap, playing only the notes immediately before and after it. Instruct her to look directly at the marked key and keep her focus there until she has landed. Once this movement becomes more confident, ask her to practice the whole section in which the leap occurs, or about a bar (measure) either side of the movement.

At home

This exercise is easily transferred directly to home practice.

Give or loan your student whatever marker you used in the lesson and instruct her to repeat the same process, first practicing just the leap in isolation, and then the full section. When she plays the complete piece through she can take the marker away, but she should still imagine it and direct her attention toward it just before the leap.

Crash Landing

In lesson

Some students with *leap phobia* are simply afraid of making a "mistake". Many students perceive correct pitch to be the most important element of piano playing, at the expense of everything else. When preparing for a leap with this mindset, they will of course slow down to be sure they don't play a wrong note.

To get over this hurdle we need to remove the element of pitch from the equation altogether. Ask your student to play her piece as normal up to the leap but then 'Crash Land' directly after the leap by flopping her hand down in roughly the right region of the keyboard. If your student is maintaining too much control over this movement, take her away from the piano and practice flopping her arms heavily down by her sides.

Continue the 'Crash Landing' exercise until your *leap phobic* student is really letting her arm fall heavily into the keys after the change in position. Once she is moving freely, ask her to return to the music as written, keeping the same feeling of flopping into the keys.

At home

During her practice time, your student should start by lifting and flopping her arms down by her sides before sitting at the piano. She should first practice her 'Crash

Landing' leap and then the note-accurate leap, before playing the piece from the beginning. Write these four steps out on her music so she doesn't forget (or download sheets with these steps at *www.pianophysician.com/bonus*).

RELATED DIAGNOSES

Finger Fascination *page 11*

4

Octave Disorientation
The confounding of notes with the same name in different octaves

Octave disorientation is an affliction that can sometimes bewilder piano teachers. As a fluent note reader, it can be difficult to see how a student could mix up a B beside Middle C with a B way down below Low C. These notes look so clearly different on the staff – how could a student confuse them?

What we need to understand is that the student with *octave disorientation* is most likely not seeing the grand staff the same way we are: as a map of the keyboard. At this stage in their learning, they do not see the logic behind the music notation system; they only see it as individual notes to be deciphered into letters. They may have memorised note names and learned how to find notes on the keyboard, but they have not really understood the underlying relationships. To cure *octave disorientation*, therefore, we need to give them a new way to look at the staff.

SYMPTOMS

• Playing in seemingly random octaves.

- Confusion about the difference between notes in different octaves.
- The belief that all notes of the same name are exactly the same.

PRESCRIPTIONS

C Reorientation

In lesson

The landmark Cs can be a fantastic grounding tool to help students with *octave disorientation*. You may already use these notes as a method of note reading, but even if you teach using a different note reading method they can still be used for this purpose. The best thing about this prescription is that it's completely universal and can be applied by your student to any piece of music.

At the start of your student's music, before the first note, draw the six Cs. These six Cs are often known as: Low C, Bass C, Middle C (one in treble clef and one in bass clef), Treble C and High C. If your student's music does not have a large note range you may be able to leave out Low C and High C. Do not, however, draw the Cs in only one clef; it's important that your student sees the symmetry in the grand staff.

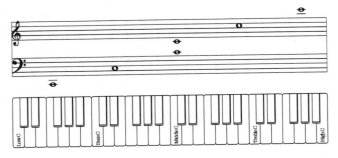

Ask your student to find each C in turn on the piano, first from bottom to top, then from top to bottom, and then randomly. Once this drill is completed, ask her for her starting note in the left hand, and to tell you which C that is closest to. Repeat this for the right hand and then allow her to begin playing. If she loses her octave orientation midway through, stop and repeat the 'C Reorientation' process, this time asking her to draw the Cs herself.

At home

You can simply leave the Cs drawn on her music to help her orientate herself at home. The six Cs will serve as a reminder that she needs to be extra careful over her octave orientation at that point in the music.

If your student has severe *octave disorientation* you might ask her to stop at each of those spots to carefully review her Cs and find her position before continuing. You may also want to assign flashcards, apps or worksheets of the landmark Cs if she does not know them well enough.

Sideways Look

In lesson

The 'Sideways Look' attempts to tackle your student's misunderstanding of the staff head-on by literally giving them a new way to see it. This method is best done with the aid of a photocopier or scanner. Your local office supply store should be able to do this for you very cheaply if you do not have access to one.

Enlarge your student's music so that one bar (measure) is at least the size of half a page or more – in many cases a 400% enlarge setting on the photocopier will work nicely. Copy a few different bars in this way, perhaps three or four places where your student often gets confused about which octave she should play in.

Put one of these bars on the music stand sideways, so that the treble clef is to the right and the bass clef to the left. Discuss with your student how the inventors came up with the grand staff idea by thinking of a keyboard on its side (a white lie). With the keyboard on its side, all the notes on the right of the piano would be up in the air, and the notes on the left would be down on the ground.

After this discussion, draw a note on your photocopied giant bar of music (keeping it on its side) and ask your student to play it on the piano. Do this for several notes and then flip the music back to its regular orientation. Point at random to each note you drew and ask your student to identify them again on the piano. Repeat these steps for each of your other photocopied bars. You may wish to break this exercise up by playing a piece or doing another lesson activity in between each bar, as interleaved practice of any concept is generally more effective and your student will be more engaged.

Repeat the 'Sideways Look' at a few subsequent lessons and the relationship of "up" on the grand staff to "right" on the keyboard – and "down" to "left" – will reveal itself to your student. Once she has grasped this internal logic she will never again confound a Low C with a Middle C or a Bass A with a Treble A.

At home

'Sideways Look' is best done in the lesson. However, you may wish to assign some other theory work (apps, worksheets, flashcards) that focuses on matching the staff directly to the keyboard as a complement to this exercise. You can then repeat 'Sideways Look' in each lesson, choosing different pieces to enlarge until your student's *octave disorientation* seems to be cured.

RELATED DIAGNOSES

❧ Finger Fascination *page 11* ❧

5

I-played-it-better-at-home-itis
The insistence that in-lesson playing doesn't properly reflect one's practice

I-played-it-better-at-home-itis is a common affliction in many music teaching studios. Although it is often true that the student did play it better at home (after all, it's more difficult to play with someone watching you), there is another side to this story.

Most students with this affliction also have a distorted view of how practice really works. When they are practicing it feels like each time they play they are improving, and that the latest repetition is the one that counts. They expect to play the piece the next time in the same quality as that last repetition, when really it might come out more like an average of all the repetitions. Practice is not a steady upward progression but rather a winding road with many twists and turns.

SYMPTOMS

• Saying the phrase "I played this better at home!" or any variation on that theme.

- Bewilderment at the mistakes one makes in the lesson.
- Confusion about how such good practice could have vanished from one's fingers.

PRESCRIPTIONS

Tallies

In lesson

If you suspect the underlying problem is that the student has an inaccurate view of her practice time, try making a little tally of the practice attempts. In the lesson, ask her to play one small section of the piece and score out of 10 how accurately it was played. (It's better that your student do this, but if she is struggling you can help her at first.)

Repeat this process 10 times with the same section. Work out the average score by adding all the scores up and dividing by 10. This average score is a more accurate representation of how well she knows that section than just the 10th score. Reassure her that if she keeps practicing the average score will go up – the practice just has to be regular and needs a check-up from time to time.

At home

Divide the piece into sections for your student. Tell her to work on just one section at a time – using 'Tallies'. She may work on more than one section a day, depending on the time she has and the length and difficulty of the sections. Her goal should be to get each section up to an average score of at least 9 out of 10.

To make this process easier for your student to follow and help her track her progress, I have created 'Tallies' tracking charts which you can download and print at: *www.pianophysician.com/bonus*.

Simulate Nervousness

In lesson

Sometimes the issue with *I-played-it-better-at-home-itis* is not one of an inaccurate view of practice but rather is caused by pure nervousness. Playing for ears other than our own (even our teacher's) can be a daunting task.

Discuss with the student how, as pianists, we have to deal with nerves if we want to play for others, take exams, compete or perform in concerts. While we can't get rid of these nerves, we need to learn to cope with them. Explain how the best way to do that is to expose ourselves to more opportunities to play when we are nervous.

At home

Give your student assignments that will put her practice to the test before the lesson. Ask her to video-record or audio-record her playing, play for family or play for her dolls. The key is to come up with regular performance opportunities so she can practice being nervous.

You might even ask your student to send you some of these recordings. Not only will you get an insight into how practice is going, but she might be less nervous to play in the lesson knowing you have already heard her play the piece during the week.

RELATED DIAGNOSES

❧ Start Again Syndrome *page 9* ☙
❧ Finger Hiccups *page 24* ☙
❧ Obstacle Sneezes *page 59* ☙

ᨏᨏᨏ 6 ᨏᨏᨏ

Finger Hiccups

The habitual repeating of a note or series of notes several times before proceeding

Most piano teachers will have a pet name for this habit. In an effort to buy thinking time, or double-check a note, students with *finger hiccups* will play the same note over and over before continuing forward. To the observer it appears almost as if the student is caught somehow on these notes and must free themselves before moving on.

These pesky hiccups can really disrupt the flow of the music and prevent the listener from enjoying a performance. The underlying causes of *finger hiccups* can be quite varied, but for the most part it tends to come down to one of two things: lack of confidence or absent-minded practice habits.

Symptoms

- Repeated notes (or repeated short sections) dotted throughout one's playing.
- Repetitive playing of notes that seems compulsive or unintentional.
- Backtracking over notes seemingly involuntarily.
- Attempting to fix notes that were played correctly.

Prescriptions

Super Slow Motion

In lesson

Tell your student that you're going to practice their piece

in 'Super Slow Motion' (if you omit the "super" 98% of students will not play slowly enough). The rules for playing in 'Super Slow Motion' are as follows:

1. You must play everything exactly as you would at full tempo including dynamics, articulation and accurate rhythms.
2. You must play as slowly as possible – the slower the better.
3. You cannot go back at any point, only forward.

If your student has trouble playing slowly, try demonstrating for her first and asking her to repeat after you. If she still can't keep a consistent slow tempo try playing alongside her, either at a second piano or in another octave on the one piano.

At home

Only assign 'Super Slow Motion' practice once your student has been successful with it during the lesson. When practicing at home using this method she should alternate playing the piece in 'Super Slow Motion' and at a regular practice tempo. The regular tempo does not need to be the full performance tempo; it's best if it is about halfway between the slow tempo and the performance tempo. She might do this alternating practice one section at a time or for the complete piece, depending on what stage she is at in the learning process and the difficulty level of the piece.

Cover Up

In lesson

Grab a small piece of paper: about 5 cm x 10 cm (2 in x 4 in) should work well for most music books. Ask your student to begin playing and, as she plays, cover the bar (measure) she is playing so that she can only see what is coming next. Repeat this exercise several times.

Stubborn *finger hiccups* can persist even while 'Cover Up' technique is being used. However, over time the 'Cover Up' exercise can help to redirect your student's eyes forward on the music. Once she is looking ahead she will be more prepared for what's coming and less likely to repeat notes just to buy thinking time.

At home

Unless a parent or someone else is helping out at home, it's unlikely that the student will be able to use the 'Cover Up' technique at home. She can, however, use the imaginary version. Ask your student to imagine that piece of paper moving over her music as she practices at home. She can't look back; it's as if the notes are vanishing as they're played. Write a reminder on your student's music about the imaginary 'Cover Up' (or better yet – have her write it herself).

RELATED DIAGNOSES
Obstacle Sneezes *page 59*
Line Limp *page 65*

7

Instant Memorisation
The almost immediate playing from memory

On the face of it this might not look like a practice ailment; it may look like a blessing. However, if you've experienced *instant memorisation* in action you will have seen the havoc it can wreak on students' reading skills and overall musical fluency.

You see, these students are not actually memorising fully and effectively but rather attempting to play by a combination of memory and ear as soon as they can. There will be many errors in their playing, and it's unlikely that they will have observed all the details of the score. What you will hear is more like a rough idea or sketch of the original piece.

Quite often, *instant memorisation* is a compensation for reading difficulties – although of course it only makes the problem worse in the long run. To get these *instant memorisers* back on track we need to simultaneously embrace their skilled musical ears and provide situations where reading is the easier option.

Symptoms

- Attempting to play from memory very early in the learning process.
- Playing from memory unconsciously or unintentionally.
- Weak reading skills that are being disguised by well-trained ears.

Prescriptions

Score Spruce-up

In lesson

In order to put your student's eyes to work before her ears can step in, you need to put the observation stage ahead of the playing stage. Select about eight pieces that you are planning to assign to your student soon, either sheet music or pieces from a book you haven't given to her yet.

Photocopy the pieces and write instructions on a sticky note for her to do the 'Score Spruce-up'. The instructions could be, for example:

1. Circle all the C chords in green.
2. Draw blue boxes around any scale passages.
3. Draw red lines between any intervals of more than a third.
4. Write the key signature at the top of the page.
5. Translate the dynamics at the bottom of the page.

Get creative with the tasks, finding assignments that will help her to see the patterns and sequences in the music. Prepare at least two of these score studies before the lesson, with different tasks for the different pieces. Help her to complete one of these 'Score Spruce-ups' in the lesson but do not ask her to play the piece yet.

At home

Assign one or more 'Score Spruce-ups' for homework, continuing to assign her other work as normal. When she brings back the spruced-up scores, take them from her, file them away, and give her some new pieces with tasks to complete. On the third week, give her some of the pieces she has already spruced up but this time with different tasks at the top.

All of this is preparation for when you eventually do assign her these pieces to practice. You can introduce a piece for playing purposes when you have collected at least three different 'Score Spruce-ups' from your student for that piece. Review all the spruced-up scores with her, talking about the different things she has marked and coloured. Then give her a clean version and start to work on playing it. Continue this process until all eight pieces have been studied and practiced, and take note of whether the *instant memorisation* is cured or needs further intervention.

Easy As Pie

In lesson

Find a book for your student which is at least a few levels below her current assignments. Look for one that does not have familiar melodies – even better if the melodies are in unusual scales or modes. Bartók's *Mikrokosmos*, for instance, would be a good choice. Be a little sneaky and tell your student that you'll be exploring this new book together as a way to learn about technique, world music, the composer, or any reason other than "to improve your reading level".

Take the first piece and work together to analyse the score (the steps, skips, leaps, note names, rhythm, key signature, etc.). Treat this music much like you might a sightreading exercise; the only difference is that your student will be practicing this for one week. Have her play through the piece with you once in the lesson, and then assign it for practice at home.

At home

Your student should practice this 'Easy As Pie' piece much like any other. In the next lesson, have her play the piece once and quickly review the mistakes and re-analyse it together. Ask her to play the piece once more and then mark the assignment complete. Start on the next 'Easy As Pie' assignment immediately.

Each 'Easy As Pie' piece only gets one week of practice, no matter what standard it reaches. The reason for this is that the pieces should be at an almost sightreadable level, so that even if your student does not practice them at home she is still getting sightreading practice in the lesson each week.

When we take away catchy melodies and long practice periods in this way, we make reading the easiest option left. Over time your student will realise this and her reading will catch up with her playing. If you want to speed up the process, you can assign multiple 'Easy As Pie' pieces each week, and/or take a hiatus from the rest of her repertoire. Be careful not to demoralise your student however by pushing her too far too quickly; one to three 'Easy As Pie' pieces is a good fit for most students.

Related Diagnoses

I-played-it-better-at-home-itis *page 21*
Finger Hiccups *page 24*
Articulation Anaemia *page 73*
Dynamic Deficiency *page 75*
Fingering Forgetfulness *page 83*

PART TWO

Part Two

≈ Fevers & Chills ≈
AKA Tempo Issues

"The tempo is the suitcase. If the suitcase is too small, everything is completely wrinkled. If the tempo is too fast, everything becomes so scrambled you can't understand it."
Daniel Barenboim

Do not confuse the tempo issues here with the beat and rhythm difficulties in Part 3. FEVERS AND CHILLS affect purely the speed at which students practice. Students with tempo issues do not have trouble understanding or producing rhythms accurately, and they can have a good sense of the beat. Fever and chill viruses usually spread to all assignments equally, and can wreak havoc on many other areas of students' playing, such as technique, note accuracy and, indeed, rhythm accuracy.

One of the key things that most students suffering with fever have failed to fully grasp is the difference between practice and performance. These students want or expect their practice to sound like a recording on the first try, and they do not understand practice time as the work that goes in to achieving the performance standard. Similarly, pianists with a chill have overlooked the work they need to put in in the practice room to get a piece up to tempo; they suppose it will fall into place quite naturally rather than being a conscious effort.

In this portion of *The Piano Practice Physician's Handbook* I will lay out some of the most widely spread viruses and some simple, homemade remedies for their effective cure. Be on the lookout for early symptoms of these maladies, and your studio will be full of steadily paced, efficient practicers.

8

Presto Infatuation
The aversion to playing slowly

This is a very common affliction indeed. *Presto infatuation* is traditionally known to manifest more in boys, although many girls also suffer from this condition. The student with *presto infatuation* does not see the point, relevance, or enjoyment to be found in playing a piece at a slow or moderate tempo.

Presto infatuation and *vivace influenza* are very easy to confuse with each other. The main difference will be found in the student's expression, body language and small utterances. When asked to play slowly, does the student groan, complain or plead with you? If they are merely reluctant to play slowly because they don't like it, yet can do so with ease when they try, then they probably have *presto infatuation*, not *vivace influenza*.

SYMPTOMS

- Distaste for playing at a slow tempo.
- Refusal to play slowly.
- Consistently practicing far too fast at home.

PRESCRIPTIONS

Aural Storytelling

In lesson

Your student with *presto infatuation* may not see the value in music that is slow. She may have a competitive nature, and have come to associate fast playing with virtuosity and skill. Playing piano could mean "winning" piano to her, and winning piano may translate in her head to playing as quickly as possible. One way to counteract this is to help the student understand the stories and feelings behind music.

Begin by listening together in lessons to recordings of music that is descriptive of something specific. Pieces that describe animals, stories or scenes are particularly easy for children to connect to. Discuss how the music was composed to represent the imagery. What dynamics, tempo and articulations did the composer utilise? Understanding the descriptive power of music can help the student connect to music in a non-competitive way.

At home

Assign additional listening exercises for the student to complete at home. Ask her to come back to you with her thoughts about the pieces: why the composer made the choices they did and what they could have done differently. Gradually, over time, you can start to apply these ideas to the music she is playing herself. What is this music about? What could the story behind it be? What tempo would fit with that description?

Social Proof

In lesson

Show your student a virtuosic pianist on YouTube playing a flashy piece. 'Flight of the Bumblebee' or the 'Minute Waltz' would both be good choices. Ask your student how she thinks this fantastic performance was achieved: how did she or he practice in order to play that quickly?

Demonstrate for her how a concert pianist would begin learning 'Flight of the Bumblebee' (or whichever piece you chose). If you have the music, open it up and show the student how a first practice session with this piece would sound, breaking it down and slowly working through a small section in front of her, just as you would practice it if you were to work on it yourself. Help her to see that slow practice is necessary for any piece, no matter how quickly it will be played in a concert.

RELATED DIAGNOSES

Vivace Influenza *page 37*

Vivace Influenza *page 37*

9

Vivace Influenza
The inability to play at a slow tempo

This practice issue is not extremely common. Students with *vivace influenza* can get stuck playing a piece at one tempo – fast. Once this speed is established, the student will have great trouble playing at a slow tempo. This quick tempo lockdown sometimes happens to all, and sometimes only a few, pieces from the student's repertoire.

The student with *vivace influenza* is having trouble playing slowly. Although *vivace influenza* and *presto infatuation* may appear similar at first, upon closer inspection you will be able to deduce whether the student can't play slowly or doesn't want to play slowly. They may complain about playing slowly or try to avoid it, but the underlying cause is one of difficulty with *vivace influenza*.

SYMPTOMS

• Altered rhythm, incorrect notes or other inaccuracies when attempting to play more slowly.

- Steady beat at one tempo becomes uneven once the tempo is changed.
- Objections to playing at a tempo other than the performance tempo.
- Comments that it's easier to play the piece more quickly.

PRESCRIPTIONS

Reverse Metronome Ladder

In lesson

We often use the metronome to help students achieve a quick tempo. For the student with *vivace influenza*, however, the reverse may be useful. Start by assessing what tempo the student is currently playing at and have her play a section of the piece with the metronome at this tempo. Next, adjust the metronome mark down 3-5 bpm and have her repeat the section at this tempo. Continue this process until you are below the tempo you wish your student to practice at, or until she gets frustrated with the process.

At home

Ask your student to adjust this process slightly for home practice. She will likely not have the patience for as many repetitions as you did together in the lesson, but she can do a modified version over several days.

For the modified version your student should begin at the tempo she is comfortable playing at, and repeat, getting a little slower each time. Assign how many times she should repeat the section (3-5 times is normally best). The next day she should repeat the same exercise, this time starting at the second last tempo she used the previous day. The table below will give you an idea of how one section might progress over five days of practice.

	1st bpm	2nd bpm	3rd bpm	4th bpm	5th bpm
Mon.	100	97	94	91	88
Tue.	91	88	85	82	79
Wed.	82	79	76	73	70
Thu.	73	70	67	64	61
Fri.	64	61	58	55	52

Download and print 'Reverse Metronome Ladder' tracking charts like this one at: _www.pianophysician.com/bonus_.

Copycat

In lesson

Play a short section of the student's piece at a slow tempo. Play the same section again, this time asking her to play along with you. Stick to your chosen speed rigidly; do not get swayed by your student's playing. (If you don't have two pianos you can play an octave lower while she plays an octave higher.) Repeat this process for the same section a few times, and then ask her to play the section on her own. Move through the piece in this way, one section at a time.

At home

If you feel your student will not be able to reliably play each section slowly at home after the in-lesson exercise, try recording each part for her to play along with. Use a smartphone, iPad or other device to quickly record each section during the lesson and email it to the student or her parents for use during practice.

Related Diagnoses

Presto Infatuation *page 35*

10
Allegro Anxiety
The fear of playing faster than moderato

I have found *allegro anxiety* to be more common in adult students, and in shy, nervous or quiet children. This fear of playing quickly is often rooted in a fear of making a mistake. Students who associate playing incorrect notes with negative feelings or punishments may never want to let go enough to play allegro.

It's admirable to want to play a note-accurate performance, but it can get in the way of the student's sense of freedom at the keys. By never playing beyond a moderate speed, not only is much of the repertoire unavailable to the student, but they can also never experience what it is to let go and allow the surge of adrenaline to carry them through a performance.

Symptoms

- Never increasing one's tempo beyond 100 bpm.
- Stress or worry about playing quickly.
- Reluctance to play quickly even when one knows a piece well.
- Stopping any time a wrong note is played.

Prescriptions

Metronome Ladder

In lesson

The metronome can be a great aid in the conquering of *allegro anxiety*. By steadily increasing the tempo just a few marks at a time, the student is untroubled by the gradual increase and can eventually get all the way up to the performance tempo.

Begin with a small section of the piece at a tempo the student is very comfortable playing at; 60 bpm is often a good starting point. After each successful play-through, increase the tempo by 3-5 bpm. If the student struggles at a new tempo for three attempts, decrease the tempo.

You'll find that at some point the student will plateau and the tempo will hover back and forth around a certain bpm mark. Take a note of this tempo on the music at this point and give your student her practice instructions.

At home

Assign 'Metronome Ladder' work to one or more sections of a piece the student is working on. The student can use the 'Metronome Ladder' without much alteration at home, although younger students will need the help of an adult to set the metronome.

The student should begin each day with the metronome set 5 bpm higher than the previous day's starting tempo. She should then proceed to repeat the section she is working on, increasing by 3-5 bpm each time. Once she plateaus she can make a note of the final tempo for that day and move on to other practice. The table below will give you an idea of how one section might progress over five days of practice.

	Starting Tempo	*Tempo Increases*	*Plateau Tempo*
Sat.	60 bpm	5 bpm	80 bpm
Sun.	65 bpm	3 bpm	83 bpm
Mon.	70 bpm	5 bpm	85 bpm
Tue.	75 bpm	3 bpm	93 bpm
Wed.	80 bpm	3 bpm	98 bpm

You can find printable 'Metronome Ladder' tracking charts like this one at: <u>*www.pianophysician.com/bonus*</u>.

Duet Sightreading

In lesson

This prescription may make some anxious students very uncomfortable so use your best judgment to read your particular student's demeanour and reactions. Make sure you pick out a level of duet that is very easy for your student. Choose a book that is several levels below her current playing level.

Explain to your student that you're going to be playing these duets together just to get a rough idea of how they sound. You might tell her that these are new books that you can't find recordings of, and you'd love her help sounding them out since you can't play them by yourself. Tell her it doesn't matter if every note is right or not, only that you don't stop or go back but keep going the whole way to the end.

One of the most important lessons from 'Duet Sightreading' comes after you have finished playing. If you slip or fudge over a few notes – as you likely will when sightreading – ask her whether she noticed you making any mistakes during the playing. Does she know where you played some wrong notes?

Have a discussion about why it still sounded good despite those mistakes, and how you kept going at the fast tempo in spite of those errors. Your student can learn a lot from seeing how even an advanced pianist makes mistakes when playing quickly, and how easily you can laugh it off. Continue this sightreading duet practice at every lesson and your student's mindset might just start to shift enough to throw caution to the wind with her regular repertoire.

Related Diagnoses

Leap Phobia *page 14*
Finger Hiccups *page 24*
Tempo Shivers *page 43*
Line Limp *page 65*

11

Tempo Shivers
Sudden and unplanned tempo changes

Even with a good sense of the beat and metre, students may unknowingly speed up or slow down at various parts of a piano piece. These *tempo shivers* can be subtle or extreme, frequent or infrequent.

Tempo shivers are most frequently caused by difficult sections, a fingering issue, or a section that is not as well rehearsed as the rest of the piece. To resolve these types of *tempo shivers* we must first resolve the underlying issue, before retraining the ear to the correct and consistent tempo of the piece.

Symptoms

- Sudden changes in tempo at a difficult section.
- Gradually decreasing or increasing in tempo during a piece.
- Starting too quickly to be able to maintain the same tempo throughout.

Prescriptions

Hands Off

In lesson

Mark each point where the student is slowing down. Ask her to answer various questions about this section without touching the keys. What fingering is she using in the right hand? And the left hand? What are the note names? What are the intervals, both melodic and harmonic? Can she sing the melody for you? How about the harmony?

Allow her to play the section once, then take away the book and ask her similar questions again. (You can download a list of sample questions at: *www.pianophysician.com/bonus*.) How much can she remember about that section? If she intellectually knows the section well, then the problem will most likely lie in her muscle memory or aural memory of that section. If this is the case, the following prescription, 'Build a Band', should be your next move.

At home

If there was a particular question or thinking point that was a stumbling block in the lesson, highlight this question for her to ask herself (or her parents to ask her) at home during practice time. Put a sticky note or write in pencil beside each section to prompt the thinking process at home. Often this is as simple as writing "Fingering?"

or "Chord changes?" on the score, and it can make all the difference to encourage effective and thoughtful home practice sessions.

Build a Band

In lesson

There is a reason why piano students are often less rhythmic than students of other instruments: early on, other instrumentalists will get many more opportunities to play with other musicians. As piano teachers, we need to put in a little more effort to create the band experience that our students are missing out on.

One easy way to do this is to have your student play with a rhythm backing track. When your student has to play along with a rhythm section, she can't change the tempo midway through the piece. The drumbeat will stay the same throughout, so if she wants to slow it down she is forced to choose a slower tempo and start again.

There are many options for you to use as a rhythm track. You can use apps such as iReal Pro or Super Metronome Groovebox. You can even find drumming tracks on YouTube in any tempo and any style you could wish for.

At home

Whichever rhythm track route you choose to go down in the lesson, make sure your student knows how to access the tracks at home. Encourage her to practice along with her new rhythm band at home as much as possible.

RELATED DIAGNOSES

∽ Leap Phobia *page 14* ∾
∽ Finger Hiccups *page 24* ∾
∽ Obstacle Sneezes *page 59* ∾
∽ Line Limp *page 65* ∾

PART THREE

Part Three

Heart Palpitations
AKA Beat & Rhythm Inconsistencies

> *"Life is about rhythm. We vibrate, our hearts are pumping blood, we are a rhythm machine, that's what we are."*
> **Mickey Hart**

Many otherwise fantastic piano students will struggle with or neglect the area of rhythm accuracy. Whether they don't see the value of rhythm or find it challenging, the result is often pianists who are less proficient in this area than other musicians. Since most piano students are not required to play in groups as frequently or as early on in their music studies, these problems can persist well beyond the beginning stages if we do not take a very proactive approach to encouraging good rhythmic fluency.

The following six beat and rhythm difficulties will

cover the majority of the overarching problems. You can use these diagnoses and prescriptions to get your students up to a good level of proficiency in this area. If you encounter problems other than the ones mentioned here, you will all the same likely find that they are related to or stemming from one of these six core issues. You can then take inspiration for their cure from the prescriptions here.

12

Restlessness

The neglecting of rest values when counting

Beyond the comprehension of rest notation, some students lack the courage to embrace silences in the music. It takes a strong will to hold a rest for its full value and keep the audience engaged and suspended in the moment of silence. Rests are as essential to a piece as notes are, but it's very easy for pianists to breeze through them and thus disrupt the overall effect of the music.

SYMPTOMS

- Failure to observe rests.
- Cutting rests short of their value.
- Not counting rest values carefully.

PRESCRIPTIONS

Take Action

In lesson

The action taken in 'Take Action' will depend on the duration of the rests and the counting method your student is using. If she is missing a one-beat rest, for example, a simple clap can be a perfect surrogate for silence. If the rest is longer you might come up with a sequence together that fits in with her counting, such as tapping: head–lap–shoulders–lap to signify a two-beat rest where she is counting "one and two and".

She can practice with the aid of these actions for quite a while, transitioning when you think she is ready to imagine the actions instead of physically doing them.

At home

Draw pictures or write notes on your student's score to remind her to practice with these actions at home. If she comes back the following week and plays without using the actions, ask her to repeat with the actions you discussed. Do this as many times as necessary until she includes the actions on the first try.

Freezeframe

In lesson

Ask your student to play as normal except that when she gets to the rest she must freeze mid-air while you count out the rest. Repeat this, asking her to count out loud herself during the rest. Then ask her to repeat it once more, this time counting in her head. Do this for all rests going forward until her *restlessness* is cured. Each time you start a new piece or section, ask her to search for the 'Freezeframes', mark them, and write in the counts she will need to say while she freezes.

At home

Your student can practice this at home using just the second two steps. The first time she plays her piece each day she should count out loud during the 'Freezeframes', and each time after that she should count in her head. Continue the same process at the next lesson, always reminding her to count out loud during the 'Freezeframes' on the first try so that she is clear this is not a one-off exercise. Be persistant and she will learn to practice this skill at home.

RELATED DIAGNOSES

Presto Infatuation *page 35*
Rhythm Allergy *page 56*

13

Beam Fever
The quickening of one's pace whenever one sees beamed notes

Quavers (eighth notes) can sometimes induce a special type of fever in the piano student's mind. When a student has *beam fever*, beamed notes are seen as a license to put the pedal to the metal. Piano teachers can be all too familiar with hearing the dreaded phrase: "These are the quick ones, right?" emerge from our students' angelic mouths.

The danger with *beam fever* is that students no longer think of the rhythm in precise, specific terms, but simply in terms of fast and slow. When they think in this way, they see those beams and play as quickly as they possibly can, no matter what their overall tempo may be.

SYMPTOMS

- Sudden bursts of speed when playing quavers (eighth notes).
- A loss of established tempo whenever beamed notes are seen.
- Random, unevenly divided beats when playing quavers or semiquavers (sixteenth notes).

PRESCRIPTIONS

Become a Lyricist

In lesson

Play the rhythm of the section with the errant quavers (eighth notes) for your student several times. Then, clap it several times and ask her to clap it with you. Do not count or use any other method to describe the rhythm.

Ask your student what words she thinks might fit with the rhythm. Some students will immediately have something that comes to mind, but others will be less sure. If she is having difficulty coming up with words ask her what her favourite food, sport or subject in school is and help her to compose lyrics for the rhythm using that topic. Since she has chosen the subject she will still feel ownership, even if you made some of the decisions for her.

Once you have the lyrics, write them into the score in pencil. If a rhythm is repeated (even with different notes) use the same lyrics for each repetition throughout the piece. Then, ask your student to clap the rhythm with you while saying the words. Next ask her to repeat the clapping and speaking once more, this time on her own.

When she is confident saying the lyrics and clapping, transfer this to just one note on the piano. Use the same process you used for the clapping exercise by first demonstrating playing and speaking for the student, then repeating together, and then asking her to repeat alone.

Finally, return to the actual music, repeating the same process of demonstration, together, then student alone. This time you can sing the lyrics, but don't worry if your student still prefers to only speak the words.

At home

This whole process can be distilled quite simply for practice time. Write the words "CLAP – ONE NOTE –

PLAY" at the top of the piece, or on a sticky note. Tell your student she has to repeat this structure she followed in the lesson using the lyrics you wrote together each time she practices. She must do this before playing the whole piece through.

Relative Rhythms

In lesson

Sometimes students with *beam fever* have simply misunderstood how the note values work. For young students, fractions may still be a foreign and confusing concept, causing them to reduce the information down to: quavers (eighth notes) = play as fast as I can.

Visual aids can do wonders to make the relationships between the different note values more apparent. The crucial thing with these visual representations is that the ratio of one note value to another be very clear. A crotchet (quarter note) should be double the width of a single quaver (eighth note) and the same width as a pair of quavers (eighth notes). Building blocks or different sized cards will work equally well. If you would like a pre-made set of cards you can find them free at: *www.pianophysician.com/bonus*.

Ask your student to construct her rhythm using the blocks or cards. Question her about how big the quavers are. How many of these could we fit inside one of those minims (half notes)? Practice clapping the rhythm with her using your preferred counting or syllable system.

At home

For her assignment that week, your student should create a drawing that is a representation of her piece.

She can use different blocks of colour for each note value, making sure that the crotchets are twice as long as the quavers, and that the minims are twice as long as the crotchets. You may want to start this exercise in the lesson and ask her to complete it at home.

RELATED DIAGNOSES

Rhythm Allergy *page 56*
Presto Infatuation *page 35*

14

Rhythm Allergy
The complete lack of a rhythmic sense

From time to time you will come across a student who is, for all intents and purposes, allergic to rhythm. These students do not just have difficulty with certain rhythm patterns or trouble playing with an even tempo; they actually pay almost no attention to note values. If they do count, they do so at random speeds, slowing down and speeding up erratically.

Whether they don't understand or don't see the relevance of playing with good rhythm is often unclear. Occasionally they will echo a rhythm back to you correctly but the next time they play that part it will have become unrecognisable once again. Don't despair. These students can learn to play with good rhythm.

SYMPTOMS

- Inconsistent rhythms within repetitions.
- Unreliable sense of note values and pulse.
- Consistent confusion over the same rhythmic pattern.

PRESCRIPTIONS

Rhythm 101

In lesson

To get to the root of the allergy, you need to take it back to the beginning. You need to know at what point your student becomes allergic to correct rhythms. Is she misunderstanding the note system? Is she simply having difficulty with the fine motor coordination?

Follow the steps laid out below before starting any new piece for several weeks in a row. Demonstrate each step for your student and then ask her to do it on her own.

1. Tap the rhythm of a short section with no reference to the written music.
2. Vocalise the rhythm (counting or using syllables) and point to the notes as you say them.
3. Play the rhythm of a section on any one note.
4. Play a section one hand at a time, as written, while vocalising the rhythm.
5. Tap the rhythm of a section using both hands, and coordinating them as they would be played.
6. Play a section hands together while vocalising the rhythm.

There may be one or several of these steps where your student struggles or falls down. Pay attention and note which exercise is most difficult for her over several weeks. This will help you to get an idea of the root cause of her *rhythm allergy*.

At home

Once you have decided what the problem area is, you can

assign extra drills, apps or worksheets that address the key problem without wasting time on other areas of rhythmic comprehension. For example, if your student is fine with all the other steps but struggles once the hands are put together, you can now address this issue by reducing the notes in one hand, using tapping drills, or assigning worksheets with two rhythm lines to follow. Having the right information will allow you to hone in on the problem area.

Unison Immersion

In lesson

Sometimes your student with a *rhythm allergy* is also rhythm indifferent. Not only does she have trouble with rhythm, but she doesn't think it's important either. If your student doesn't see the relevance of rhythm and how integral it is to music, it's likely that no amount of drills or special techniques will help her, except perhaps total immersion.

In a different octave on the same piano – or on a second piano if you have one – play all your student's music in unison with her. Don't allow yourself to get swayed by her rhythms; stick rigidly to the precise rhythmic structure of the piece. This will mean playing much more slowly than she normally plays, and most likely in short sections to help her to focus.

She may be very resistant to this way of playing at first. It will be hard work compared to her usual approach of disregarding the rhythm entirely. Stick at it and gradually she will pick up the rhythms and start to see their relevance.

To make this exercise more palatable, tell her there are dancers working on a routine to the music. Every time she gets out of sync with you, the dancers lose their footing and you need to restart that section (or the whole piece for very short pieces) so that they can practice their routine properly.

At home

You can record yourself playing for your student to play along with at home. However, if she has a severe *rhythm allergy* it's unlikely that she will follow through at first. Persist with this manner of working during lesson time and eventually she may look for the aid of a play-along track to practice with.

RELATED DIAGNOSES

～ Restlessness *page 51* ～ ～
Beam Fever *page 53* ～
～ Obstacle Sneezes *page 59* ～

～ 15 ～

Obstacle Sneezes
The propensity to pause before playing a difficult section

Many students will exhibit this distinctive pause-and-launch-forward combination at some stage in their piano studies. I liken this to a sneeze because of the characteristic time taken to freeze before exploding forward into the part of the piece that they find most difficult. Most of the time they will be completely unaware of the time they are taking to pause before proceeding into a particular section, and discussing the sneeze will only cause them to seize up even more in anticipation. A step-by-step, systematic approach is needed to cure *obstacle sneezes*.

Symptoms

- Delay or breaking of tempo before a difficult passage.
- Bracing and tensing before playing a tricky part.
- Pausing before launching forward in a resolute or determined manner.

Prescriptions

Edge Forward

In lesson

Mark the obstacle that's causing your student to sneeze. Ask her to play the preceding bar and just the first note of the obstacle. It may be helpful to mark lines or add small sticky notes to stop her from being tempted to play more than desired. Slow her tempo and repeat this method until she can successfully bring the first note in on time at least three times in a row.

Add one more note or chord at a time until she can play a few bars into or past the obstacle that she was sneezing over. Then reinforce the new behaviour by starting at the beginning of the section and playing through the obstacle a few times.

At home

The more times you reiterate and name each step involved, the more likely your student is to follow through at home. Discuss with her what's involved in 'Edge Forward' and how she could apply it to her practice. Talk about and mark other places that could benefit from this approach.

As with many other techniques it will likely take several repetitions in the lesson before she starts to use 'Edge Forward' at home. Persist, and in time it will sink in.

Edge Backward

In lesson

As you can probably tell, this prescription isn't all that different from 'Edge Forward'. However, by reversing the process we do get some different benefits. I suggest using 'Edge Forward' if you believe the *obstacle sneeze* is caused by a mental block, and 'Edge Backward' if you suspect a technical issue is the culprit.

Mark the obstacle on your student's music. Ask her to practice the full obstacle – normally one or two bars (measures). Then expand the obstacle to include one note/chord before it. Have her practice this until she can play it three times in a row successfully, and then expand the obstacle again. Continue expanding until the section being practiced is at least double the length of the original obstacle. Once this has been mastered, run through the larger section or the full piece to put the obstacle back into context.

At home

Ask your student to explain the process back to you once you have completed the 'Edge Backward' exercise. Do this many times in the lesson before asking her to practice this way at home. If you continue to summarise the process and discuss the steps involved, she may take the initiative to use the method during her practice time.

Related Diagnoses

Leap Phobia *page 14*
Finger Hiccups *page 24*
Tempo Shivers *page 43*
Line Limp *page 65*

16

Beat Arrhythmia
The lack of a sense of beat or pulse in one's playing

A good sense of pulse can carry the listener through a cacophony of wrong notes or incorrect rhythms. If the beat remains intact we can stick with a performer and barely notice they made an error but, if they lose the beat, even the least musical people in the audience will feel it in some sense.

Many students arrive to us with some feeling for the beat already baked in. However, there are a few who are behind the curve in this area whom we need to assist in finding that lost beat every time. Metronomes and counting techniques are often ineffective against *beat arrhythmia* because if the student can't feel the beat they often can't hear it either. Thus we need to find ways to get the beat inside these students, for them to feel it in their bones.

SYMPTOMS

- Slightly offbeat rhythms that are otherwise correct.
- Missing beats or changing metre where there is no change.
- An inability to tap along with the beat.

PRESCRIPTIONS

A Pat on the Back

In lesson

When metronomes don't work, sometimes you need to get a little more manual. Choose a piece your student can already play quite well, apart from the lacking sense of pulse. Set up a metronome at the tempo you would like your student to play – it will need to be very slow at first. Begin patting her on the back or shoulder in time to the metronome and then ask her to count in and start playing. Continue the patting throughout the piece, even if she strays from the beat a little.

If the 'Pat on the Back' was enough to bring her piece in line, then great! You have your cure. Just keep it up with all her pieces and try it out at lots of different tempi to let the feeling of the beat sink in.

If she still struggles to stay on time, ask her to locate where in her music each pat was. Help her find the main beats in her piece and mark them with a little 'x' in the middle of the grand staff. Once all the beats are marked, repeat the 'Pat on the Back' exercise, this time breaking it down into chunks and slowing the tempo as needed. You might try just one bar (measure) at a time at first, gradually building up to larger sections of the piece.

At home

She will not have you to pat her back at home so this may be one solution that is only for lesson time. If you have a particularly enthusiastic and involved piano parent, however, you could certainly enlist their help. Otherwise just continue working on this in the lesson and gradually wean her off the pats and onto the metronome alone. Once this is achieved she will be able to practice with the metronome at home.

Bucket Drummer

In lesson

Pick out a bucket, lunchbox, box, or anything that could work as a makeshift drum. Ask your student to tap a steady beat on this 'drum'. Tell her she can choose the tempo, but it can't get faster or slower; it has to stay exactly the same. Once her beat is established, begin to play her current piece on the piano.

If her tempo changes, stop playing. You might even crash dramatically into the keys in mock confusion. Help her to start up her beat again and then return to playing. Tell her the goal is for you to get the whole way through without having to stop and the only way to do that is if the beat stays at exactly the same speed.

Once she manages to keep the beat the whole way through the piece (even if this takes several lessons to achieve), swap places and set the beat yourself for her to play at. This time she has to get through the piece without straying from your beats.

Depending on the student, this may be motivating or frustrating. You might want to remove the quasi competitive element and simply ask her to try to stay with you as best she can for three tries, rather than looking for a perfect run. Use your judgement and your knowledge of your student's personality to decide which approach is better.

At home

During practice she can be a 'Bucket Drummer' for recordings or YouTube clips. You might even assign a playlist of YouTube clips, and tell her to identify the ones that pull her 'Bucket Drumming' faster or slower because of their wobbly tempo. This would be a great opportunity for her to notice the relevance and importance of a steady beat and might provide her with the motivation she needs.

RELATED DIAGNOSES

Tempo Shivers *page 43*
Restlessness *page 51*
Rhythm Allergy *page 56*
Line Limp *page 65*

17

Line Limp
The belief that barlines are signs for one to stop or yield

Beginner piano students can be tempted to see written music as fitting into separate little "boxes" of information. While initially this seems to them an easy way to digest all the signs and symbols, it means they don't think about the next "box" until the current "box" is completed. This separation is what causes some students to limp slowly over each barline before proceeding forward.

This problem with a pianist's gait can be very distracting. Without seeing the written music as continuous and flowing from bar to bar (measure to measure) and line to line, they cannot establish a steady and predictable pulse. The listener therefore is distracted, and is incapable of being swept up and carried away by the music.

SYMPTOMS

- Pausing at almost all barlines.
- Difficulty moving fluidly from one bar (measure) to the next.
- No sense of continuous pulse.

PRESCRIPTIONS

Plus One

In lesson

Starting at the beginning of the piece or the section with which your student is having trouble, use a sticky note to cover up the notes after the first note in the second bar (measure). Instruct your student to play just this small chunk: bar 1 plus one note from bar 2.

Once she can do this successfully without pausing, move the sticky note one bar forward, so that it now covers the notes after the first note of bar 3. Continue in this manner for about six bars and then restart the process from bar 7, then from bar 13, and so on.

At home

Depending on how this progresses during the lesson, and your student's history with *line limping*, the lesson activity may be enough to cure this ailment. If you feel the issue still needs more attention, however, try assigning this 'Plus One' exercise for just one section a day. Use your discretion: most young students will not have the stamina or the time to complete this exercise for more than a few bars in each practice session.

Forward Thinking

In lesson

Ask your student to try to keep her eyes on your pen as she plays. As she is playing stand beside her and point your pen at her music, just beyond the notes she is currently playing. Try to stay about one or two beats ahead of her playing.

Repeat this exercise a few times to encourage your student to draw her eyes forward while she's playing. You may find this is enough to cure the *line limp* right away. If it doesn't sink in immediately, don't worry. Keep at it over several weeks at every lesson and eventually she should be able to look forward and think ahead to what's coming up. Thinking ahead is the key to the long-term cure of *line limp*, and to great reading in general.

At home

Have your student make a note on her score in her own words to remind herself to continue to try to move her gaze forward at home. While most students will not be diligent enough to follow through on this advice the first week, over time it will take effect and the reminder will be enough to practice this skill.

RELATED DIAGNOSES

Finger Hiccups *page 24*
Obstacle Sneezes *page 59*

PART FOUR

PART FOUR

Vision Impairment
AKA Symbol & Marking Oversight

"It's attention to detail that makes the difference between average and stunning."
Frances Atterbury

The title of this group of piano practice ailments is, of course, a little tongue-in-cheek. Students who fail to observe the details in their music do not have any problem seeing these markings. It can sometimes seem to us teachers as if they are completely blind to dynamics, articulation, accidentals, fingering and phrase lines – however, they are simply prioritising what to pay attention to in the vast array of squiggles and lines that lies before them. After all, their teacher spends so much time helping them find the notes on the keyboard and drilling rhythms; all the other bits seem more like an afterthought.

All these additional symbols that are getting ignored, however, are a big part of what makes music sound musical. When our students miss out on this icing on the musical cake, they are missing many opportunities to flow in the music and truly delight the audience (even if the audience is just you). All of the prescriptions in the Vision Impairment section of *The Piano Practice Physician's Handbook* have been designed to not just solve the issue at hand, but to bring a sense of creativity and even whimsy into your piano studio. Help your students to see themselves as performers, musicians and artists, and you will cure their inattention to detail long-term.

18

Articulation Anaemia

The omission of all or most articulation from one's playing

Articulation is a big part of piano playing, but to a piano student it can seem like just one more thing to focus on. For the student with *articulation anaemia*, staccato marks, slurs and accents pale in comparison to notes and rhythms.

To combat *articulation anaemia* we need the student to reorder their priority list, and also to have the confidence and technical skills necessary to execute the articulation. This affliction is one not of the mind only, but of the heart too. Articulation requires conviction.

SYMPTOMS

- An absence of articulation from one's playing.
- Not seeing the relevance or importance of articulation marks.
- Half-hearted execution of articulation.

PRESCRIPTIONS

Vocalise

In lesson

One way to bring articulation to the forefront of your student's playing is to involve speech. Demonstrate the music for your student and come up with syllables together that fit the articulation used:

- Single staccato notes could be "tat".

- A series of staccato quavers (eighth notes) might then be "rat tat tat tat".
- The two-note slurs could become "yah-dah".

Write the articulation vocalisations on your student's score. Play the piece yourself and ask your student to be the vocalist. If she's shy about it you can sing along with her. Once she is comfortable saying or singing the new lyrics, ask her to play the piece while you both vocalise the articulation.

At home

Assign home practice with the vocalisations. Ask your student to also write another way to vocalise her piece. Perhaps she could even teach the new "lyrics" to her family so they can sing along while she plays?

Conduct It

In lesson

Play the piece your student is working on, either yourself or from a recording. Discuss all the articulations used and how they enhance the playing. If your student was a conductor, how could she show the musicians that she wanted this articulation?

Ask your student to act as your conductor while you play her piece. You may need to review the articulation used and where it occurs first. If the score had no articulation marks, would you know where to put certain articulations from her actions? Try the same exercise with music your student has not seen or heard before if you would like to explore articulation with her further. The more different contexts the better.

At home

Ask your student to imagine herself conducting as she plays. How would she show the staccato marks? What would she as the conductor want the player to do there? The strong visual should help her to place emphasis and importance on the articulation during her home practice.

RELATED DIAGNOSES

⤜ Expression Omission Disorder *page 93* ⤛

⤜ 19 ⤛

Dynamic Deficiency
The absence of dynamic contrast in one's playing

Dynamics is one of the most common missing ingredients from a student's playing and, without dynamic contrast, a pianist's playing is lifeless and dull. This *dynamic deficiency* is often accompanied by a perceived information overload from the student's perspective and can be exacerbated by tempo illnesses such as *vivace influenza* and *presto infatuation*. The root of *dynamic deficiency* is not in the comprehension of the signs and symbols (or if it is, it is easily addressed). The underlying problem is similar to that of *articulation anaemia*: it is either a lack of desire or a feeling of overwhelm.

SYMPTOMS

- A lack of dynamic contrast in one's playing.
- Not placing importance on dynamic marks.
- The belief that including dynamics is too difficult.

Prescriptions

Dramatise

In lesson

Have a discussion with your student about the dynamics in her piece and how they fit into the narrative of the music. Help her to come up with a possible story to accompany the music if the piece is not directly descriptive or story-telling. Playing the piece through a few times for her might help to spark her imagination – even more so if she closes her eyes.

Once you have your story, help your student to come up with actions or mimes to accompany it. (If she has played charades before you can use this as a reference.) Encourage her to jump up, crouch down and mime various actions to describe the story. Play through the piece a few times with exaggerated dynamics while she dramatises the music.

Next, ask your student to return to the piano and play her piece, imagining the full storyline as she plays. If she is still not adding all the dynamics, prompt her with questions about the story rather than the markings: "What's happening at that point there? How can the audience hear this in your playing?"

At home

Your student should continue this same imaginative practice at home, showing her family the mimes and keeping the dramatisation in her mind's eye as she practices. For further reinforcement, ask her to write down the story or draw a picture to represent it and bring it to the next lesson. Leave it up to her which she chooses so she can take ownership of the task.

Transfiguration

In lesson

Some *dynamic deficiencies* are caused by fear of embarrassment and/or a lack of confidence in one's playing. If your student is shy of being a performer, animal imagery can be a useful device to help her come out of her shell. When playing "like an elephant", for example, we allow ourselves a level of detachment from our own playing. This can give us confidence to play in the more exaggerated manner that is sometimes necessary to achieve the correct sound.

For each dynamic mark, pick an animal to use as inspiration for the playing. If your student is young, you can even use stickers or draw pictures on the score to represent each animal. Now as she is playing you can prompt her not by saying "You missed the sforzando at bar (measure) 12" but rather "Remember that's where the lion roars very suddenly". Using her playing to represent a menagerie of animals will bring a whole new meaning and playfulness to dynamic contrast for your student.

At home

If you added drawings or stickers to your student's score it will be easy for her to remember this 'Transfiguration' at home. If not, ask her to describe the animal imagery in her piece to a family member before practicing. Can they hear the lion roaring? What about that little field mouse near the end?

RELATED DIAGNOSES

❧ Expression Omission Disorder *page 93* ❧
❧ Fortissimo Fixation *page 96* ❧
❧ Pianissimo Preoccupation *page 99* ❧

༂ 20 ༂

Accidental Amnesia
The consistent overlooking of sharps and flats

Please note that within *accidental amnesia* I am including not just accidentals but sharps and flats in the key
signature also. You may have several students with *accidental amnesia* in your studio right now, and you have
probably circled, highlighted and coloured the sharps and
flats in their pieces many times over to no avail. Often,
with the best of intentions, we are actually making the
problem worse by drawing more and more attention to
the score. The real cure to *accidental amnesia* (especially
when it comes to key signatures) lies in the fingertips, not
on the page.

SYMPTOMS

- Repeatedly missing sharps and flats.
- Fingers that do not fall naturally into the new key
  signature.
- Frustration at missing accidentals that one was fully
  aware of.

PRESCRIPTIONS

Feeling Fuzzy

In lesson

This is my recommended prescription for most students
with *accidental amnesia*. In almost all cases you should
prescribe 'Feeling Fuzzy' first, and only proceed to 'The
Symbol Siren' (below) as an enhancement or fun variation. 'Feeling Fuzzy' is what will allow your student to

switch gears and transfer her attention from the page to her fingertips, and that is what will make all the difference.

Help your student to find all the white keys on the keyboard that are not used in the piece. For example, in D major you would be looking for all the Cs and Fs that come up in the piece. Place a small pompom, piece of felt, cotton wool or other soft item on each of these keys.

Ask your student to play her piece, being careful not to step on any of the fuzzies' heads. She will notice immediately if she does because of the different sensation under her fingertips. This is preferable to the aural feedback of playing the wrong note since, over time, she will learn to react quickly once she feels the top of the fuzzy surface and self-correct to play the black key instead.

At home

Give your student the fuzzies to take home with her. Before she leaves make sure to give her several opportunities to practice finding the keys that need fuzzies so she is confident setting them up at home. This will also give her another chance to navigate the key signature and accidentals in her piece. After 1-2 weeks of this practice she can most likely graduate to imaginary fuzzies, and only use the fuzzies as an aid once in a while if *accidental amnesia* starts to return.

The Symbol Siren

In lesson

This is a good choice if you feel your student is being careless and is not having genuine trouble with using accidentals. It can also act as a whimsical supplement to the 'Feeling Fuzzy' cure above. I normally do not advocate punitive styles of piano practice, however, I think 'The

Symbol Siren' can be done with an air of fun that will not make students feel as if they are being scolded. If you feel your student is very sensitive to criticism, do not use this practice technique.

Ask your student to begin playing and, every time she misses a sharp or flat, start your siren. You can use a big button (often available at dollar stores or toy stores), an app, or just your own voice if you prefer.

Whenever she hears the siren she must play the sharp or flat she missed three times, and then return to the beginning and start again. Continue this for as long as it remains fun and informative, and stop if there are any signs of anger or frustration from your student.

At home

This is one exercise that I think is best left to the imagination at home, even if you have a piano parent who would be on board. 'Symbol Sirens' can be a bit of fun with one's teacher, but with a parent it is very likely to be seen as pure chastisement. Best leave the game-show element of this prescription for the lessons. Do, however, ask your student to imagine those sirens going off at home and to follow the same procedure of repeating the note three times and returning to the beginning. And make sure she knows the sirens will be blaring again at her next lesson, so she better be prepared!

RELATED DIAGNOSES

Note Deafness *page 91*

🢒 *21* 🢐

Wrist Lockdown
The lack of wrist lifts at phrase/slur endings

Part of beautiful piano playing involves being able to shape phrases and let them breathe. Wrist lift-offs at phrase endings and in two- and three-note slurs are what give the phrases a soft tapering off and allow the piano to sing.

Students with *wrist lockdown* will continue from one phrase or slur straight to the next without any movement or break in legato, no matter how many times they are prompted by their teacher. No amount of reminding is going to help these students to form phrase endings – they require a bigger intervention.

SYMPTOMS

- No wrist movement at phrase or slur endings.
- Playing legato from one phrase or slur into the next.
- A lack of "breathing" in one's musical phrasing.

PRESCRIPTIONS

Imaginary String

In lesson

Tell your student that she is going to become a puppet, and you will be the puppeteer. Tell her there is a string tied to each of her wrists, and you are holding the other ends in each hand. Stand beside or behind her so that she can just see you in the corner of her eye, and hold out your hands to hold the "strings". Practice moving the strings around while she follows your movements with her wrists.

Once she is used to following your movements, ask her to play her piece again, continuing to act as your puppet. Shape the phrase and slur endings as they occur by "lifting" her wrists. When she finishes, discuss what you were doing – where the wrist movements were and the effect they had on the music.

At home

Carry this analogy through to your student's practice time also. Ask her to imagine she still has a puppeteer moving those strings when she reaches the end of a slur, and to practice smooth puppet-like movements for next week. You could even ask her to draw a puppet string on her music to help her remember.

Forceful Fingering

In lesson

Most of the time it's possible to build the wrist lifts right into the fingering. If you know your student is unlikely to observe the phrase lines and slurs in a new piece, carefully plan and notate the fingering she will use so that she won't have a choice but to lift and move. Of course you will still need to talk about the technique needed to smooth these movements out, but built-in fingering is sometimes the best way to go.

At home

The only instruction you need to give for practice now is to make sure she follows the fingering you have notated. If she has trouble paying attention to fingering, see the next section on *fingering forgetfulness*.

RELATED DIAGNOSES

❧ Fingering Forgetfulness *page 83* ❧

22

Fingering Forgetfulness
The ignoring of finger numbers

Some piano students will unknowingly create extra work for themselves by ignoring the finger numbers written on the score. Failing to pay attention to the annotated fingering means they will use a different fingering on each repetition, making it that much harder to gain the muscle memory needed to play fluently.

Though the opposite problem of relying too heavily on finger numbers can be present in beginner students, *fingering forgetfulness* is more common in intermediate students. By this stage they will be pretty good note readers, but are missing this other, crucial bit of information from the score.

SYMPTOMS

- Randomised fingering upon each playing.
- The use of awkward or unsuitable alternate fingerings.
- Not paying attention to notated fingerings, either printed or written-in.

PRESCRIPTIONS

Fingering Overload

In lesson

One way to fight *fingering forgetfulness* is to immerse your student in fingering. Ask her to put a finger number on her score for every single note. Help her at first and then give her more fingering notation as part of her homework.

It's important to note that this is not suitable for every student. If your student is a struggling note reader, this prescription may be a possible reading crutch that you want to avoid. However, when it is a good fit, 'Fingering Overload' can really get your student to think about the fingering she is using throughout the piece.

At home

Once the fingering is written in, your student must follow it every single time. Tell her that if she wants to change a fingering, that's fine, but it has to be changed on the score too. She's not allowed to play a fingering other than what is written in during practice or the lesson.

If you have a student with very persistent *fingering forgetfulness* try asking her to start again whenever she uses a fingering that is not written in. With this system she'll soon learn to follow the finger numbers during practice.

Finger Aloud

In lesson

Have your student play one hand at a time while saying the finger she is using out loud. Saying the finger numbers as she plays will help draw her attention to what she is really doing.

If you come across a clash between her fingering and what is notated, ask her the logic behind each choice. If she can explain why her fingering is better, then change the notated finger number; if not, then she must repeat that section with the correct fingering.

At home

Ask your student to repeat this exercise once or twice during her practice this week. This little check-in should be enough to ensure she doesn't revert to old habits between lessons.

Related Diagnoses

Finger Hiccups *page 24*

PART FIVE

Ear Infections
AKA Musical Insensitivity

"Ah, music," he said, wiping his eyes. "A magic beyond all we do here!"
Dumbledore, J.K. Rowling, Harry Potter and the Philosopher's Stone

What is music making for if we don't listen to it? I guess we could consider it a mild cardiovascular exercise regimen, a practice in discipline, or maybe a way to improve our intelligence (no, I'm not going to cite any studies or infographics on this). I think we can all agree that music is supposed to be listened to. What a shame then when our students treat it as a series of motions translated from the page to the fingers, bypassing the ears completely.

Getting to experience one's own playing and understand music in a new way through the process of getting inside the notes is one of the greatest pleasures of piano playing. It's what keeps many young piano students coming back to the instrument again and again. It can help your students stay on the bench too – if you can only open their ears in the first place.

❧ 23 ❧

Note Deafness

The inability to hear incorrect notes played by oneself

Students with *note deafness* play through a piece with wrong notes dotted about the place. They don't stop and try to fix these wrong notes or restart at the beginning – in fact they don't seem to notice them at all.

Many students with this affliction will finish playing and be perfectly happy with the way they played. They are unaware of the incorrect notes played along the way. When told about the pitch discrepancies they will often think that they played the correct notes. "You played an F here when it should be a G" might be met with "No I didn't, I did play the G!" The student may be quite insistent and resist the idea that they played a wrong note.

SYMPTOMS

- Random note inaccuracies seemingly without pattern or sequence.
- An inability to say whether a piece was played with the correct notes.
- An inability to point out which notes were played incorrectly.
- Denial that incorrect notes were played.

PRESCRIPTIONS

Sing Along

In lesson

The student who is *note deaf* sometimes has an underdeveloped sense of pitch. Ask your student to try to sing her piece for you. If she is shy or uncertain at first join in and 'Sing Along' too. You can also include the piano with both your voices.

At home

Assign your student singing practice. Ask her to 'Sing Along' with a recording of her piece (you could record it during the lesson if there isn't one readily available) each day before playing the piano. Immediately afterwards she should sing the piece on her own while pointing to the score, and only then should she go to the piano and play the piece while singing along.

Play Along

In lesson

'Play Along' with your student in a different octave. When she plays an inaccurate note she might notice the clash with the note you played. If you try this hands together to no avail, repeat the exercise one hand at a time. If she still doesn't hear the wrong notes, slow the tempo until she does hear the difference.

Try to take an inquisitive rather than correcting tone in this exercise. If you are too critical your student may be embarrassed by her mistakes, and that negative emotion could get associated with piano lessons in general. For example, you might ask your student: "Hmm, why does that sound a bit funny? I think I'm playing an F there when you played an F sharp. Let's just double check that note together."

At home

This translates best to home practice with the use of a

backing track, slowed recording, or teacher recording. You could record the piece in multiple tempi, or make use of an app to slow the tempo down to practice speed. Ask your student to practice along with the recording each day before she practices alone.

RELATED DIAGNOSES

❧ Finger Hiccups *page 24* ☙
❧ Accidental Amnesia *page 78* ☙

24

Expression Omission Disorder
The lack of expression in one's playing

After all that hard work learning the notes, analysing rhythms and conquering the technique in a piano piece, sometimes a student's performance can still fall flat. It's not surprising that expressive playing is something that piano students struggle with, however, since us teachers often leave this part until the very end. Only when our students know the piece backwards and forwards do we talk about adding feeling to their piece.

Unfortunately, this means that our students are least practiced in the art of bringing music to life for an audience. To cure *expression omission disorder*, we need to bake the artistry into the learning process – not add it as a layer of icing at the end of the learning process.

SYMPTOMS

• Accurate but expressionless playing.

- A robotic or mechanical feeling to one's playing.
- A lack of emotion or feeling behind the music.

PRESCRIPTIONS

Pick a Painting

In lesson

Discuss with your student what the story, feeling or message behind her piece might be. Talk about it in terms of historical context, composer and structure, as appropriate to your student's age and level.

Once you have come to an agreement on a backstory, discuss what type of image might describe this. Search online for a painting, photo or other visual representation of the backstory. This could be anything from a painting done during the composer's time to graffiti art of a key word that represents the piece. Remember: it needs to be something your student understands and connects to the music – so let her do the choosing.

Print out the picture and two other random images. Place the pictures on the music stand, on top of the piano, or anywhere else that will be in your student's eye-line while she is playing. Ask her to play again, this time as if trying to convey to a listener which of the images she has picked out for the piece. Tell her it should be clear to anyone listening which picture she has chosen without any words being used.

At home

Attach the image to your student's piece with a paperclip and ask her to take a moment to look at it before she plays each day. Tell her that you will be repeating the same 'Pick a Painting' exercise at the next lesson and you want it to be even clearer to the imaginary listener which one she is describing.

Gesture Gist

In lesson

This exercise is best done before your student knows a piece very well, but it can be done at any point in the learning process. Pick out three or four performances of your student's piece on YouTube/Vimeo, preferably by well-known pianists who have very different styles or approaches. If your student is playing a piece that is not recorded, you can use a piece she is not playing just as an example.

Play the videos on a device that your student can see while sitting at the piano. Ask her to imitate the general movements the pianist is making as the video plays. She shouldn't play anything on the piano but instead ghost play or play "air piano". Repeat this for each of the performers you have picked out.

At home

Assign your student practice of her piece in these three or four distinct styles. Even if her piece is different than the one she was imitating she can still replicate the style and apply it to her own piece.

If she already knows the piece quite well, challenge her to play the piece in two of the performers' styles at the next lesson in a way that will enable you to guess which performers she is imitating. If she doesn't yet know the piece, she can play air piano instead with a recording of the piece. Separating the gestures from the notes in this way is often more beneficial, as it will allow her to focus purely on the large movements and see the bigger picture.

RELATED DIAGNOSES

❧ Articulation Anaemia *page 73* ❧
❧ Dynamic Deficiency *page 75* ❧
❧ Wrist Lockdown *page 81* ❧
❧ Fortissimo Fixation *page 96* ❧
❧ Pianissimo Preoccupation *page 99* ❧

25

Fortissimo Fixation
Refusal to play at a volume other than the maximum

This issue is most common among beginners, although I have come across some students up to an intermediate level with particularly resistant forms of the disease. Many students with *fortissimo fixation* think of playing the piano as pressing buttons. They believe that if they press the right buttons at the correct time then they are playing correctly. If this is the case, it's no wonder that they press each key down so swiftly and emphatically, creating the harsh banging sound that results.

SYMPTOMS

- Unpleasantly loud playing almost all the time.
- A "heavy-handed" piano technique.
- Failure to recognise how loudly one is playing.

PRESCRIPTIONS

As Soft As...

In lesson

The trick with this remedy is to make it into a game. If

your student has *fortissimo fixation* I'm sure you have already tried asking her to play more softly. That's not what I'm suggesting here.

As soon as your student has finished playing a piece very loudly and roughly, launch right into the 'As Soft As...' activity. Don't correct anything in her piece or make comments about the dynamics but go straight to this activity just as if it were the next thing on the agenda.

Ask your student to think of the quietest thing she can. It doesn't matter what example she chooses; anything quiet will do. Once she has chosen, ask her to play something simple (a scale, piece or exercise she knows well) "as soft as a __". Encourage her to play more and more softly using the comparison she has chosen, for example: "A swan gliding on a pond is even softer, isn't it? Swans make *almost* no sound at all! Let's try that one more time."

When she has mastered playing "as soft as a __" with the simple scale or piece, return to the original piece she played for you. Phrase your directions with a sense of curiosity: "Hey, I wonder what that Gigue would sound like if it were played as quietly as that swan. Let's try that now."

At home

Assign your student practice of all her pieces like the softest things she can imagine. Ask her to draw a different example of something super quiet at the top of each page, or in her assignment book. Continue to use the words "as soft as" or "as quiet as" and avoid using musical terms such as "pianissimo". Your student might be put off by the Italian terms if she has been corrected and reminded about dynamics a lot in the past.

Freefall

In lesson

If your student's *fortissimo fixation* is rooted in a technique issue, then a great deal of 'Freefalls' may be in order. Good indicators that the problem is actually a technique problem rather than a choice include proclamations of "I just can't play any quieter!" and/or that your student appears to be pushing or forcing her way into each key.

Start away from the keys and stand facing your student. Demonstrate the 'Freefall', stretching your arms up above your head and then letting them fall down heavily by your sides. Repeat this exercise several times.

Once the 'Freefall' is well established, sit down again facing your student and demonstrate the 'Freefall', this time with your hands starting at shoulder height and dropping onto your knees.

Translate the 'Freefall' motion to the piano next, starting with just one hand playing a single key. These 'Freefalls' should still be quite exaggerated, starting from at least 60 cm (2 ft) or so above the keys. If your student's movements appear to be free from tension and she is using the natural weight of her arm, begin to apply this technique to her repertoire. Keep the notes broken apart, lifting and freefalling to play each and every note. Whether she can play hands together or separately only will be down to each individual student.

Keep an eye on her technique and, if tension returns, simplify the 'Freefall' exercise to alleviate it. She will still be playing loudly, but the arm weight will create a warm, full tone so that she can play fortissimo without harshness.

At home

Have her practice at least one piece (or possibly all her assignments) using the 'Freefall' technique this week, and check that she is still moving freely at the next lesson. Once the arm is engaged you can start to introduce other dynamics and minify the arm motions, integrating the feeling of 'Freefall' seamlessly into her playing technique.

RELATED DIAGNOSES

Expression Omission Disorder *page 93*
Sticky Tipitis *page 112*
Floppy Finger Predicament *page 121*

26

Pianissimo Preoccupation
Refusal to play at a volume other than the minimum

This affliction is less common among young children. It usually affects shy, uncertain or nervous piano students and I have found it to be very prevalent amongst older beginners. In the same way that we might speak more softly or with a quiver in our voice when speaking a foreign language, students with *pianissimo preoccupation* feel uncomfortable playing loudly, especially if they are unsure of the notes.

This fear of making a mistake prevents them from playing with conviction and ultimately inhibits their musicality. It can become a self-fulfilling prophecy: they think they won't sound musical so they play so lightly on the keys that they don't sound musical. We need to break this cycle quickly or these hesitant pianists are very likely to give up altogether.

SYMPTOMS

- Very quiet or hesitant playing.
- A touch that is too light, bouncing from the keybed as soon as it is struck.
- Expressing a fear of being overheard by neighbours or passers-by.

PRESCRIPTIONS

Roar!

In lesson

This remedy will have to be used at many consecutive lessons and every practice session for maximum effectiveness. The 'Roar!' is really very simple but can get a lot of pushback from tentative students – so be prepared to be persistent and persuasive.

Ask your student to play the first note, notes, or chord of whatever piece she is working on as a warm-up. She must play them as loudly as possible. Explain that this 'Roar!' is like clearing her throat before giving a speech. It should get the attention of the imaginary audience before she starts her piece properly or begins her other practice on that particular piece. Continue to ask for a 'Roar!' before every scale, exercise and piece throughout the lesson.

At home

Ask your student to incorporate the 'Roar!' into her daily piano practice. It must be done before every single piece, every time. Of course you cannot guarantee that she will follow through on this, but you can continue to request it at every lesson until she starts to do the 'Roar!' for you unprompted.

Hairpin Scales

In lesson

When students are overwhelmed and uncomfortable with the amount of information processing required to play the piano, often the best solution is to take away the written music. Having one less thing to focus on might be just the confidence boost your student needs to play with the boldness we're looking for.

For now, ignore your student's *pianissimo preoccupation* in her pieces and focus solely on cultivating dynamics in her warm-ups. Scales are my preferred warm-ups but you might also apply this to Czerny, Hanon, or any rote exercises. At the start of every lesson ask your student to play her scales, first with a crescendo ascending and diminuendo descending, and then the reverse. She should make these dynamics as dramatic and exaggerated as possible.

At home

Assign scale practice in the same way with extreme 'Hairpins' applied to each scale. It's important that your student practice the diminuendo ascending and crescendo descending also, so that she gets used to beginning loudly as well as working up to it.

Over time she will grow more comfortable with the full dynamic range of the piano and then you can start to discuss the dynamics in her pieces also. This may take weeks or months, but try not to rush her. Wait until she can play her scales confidently in this way, without encouragement or persuasion from you.

RELATED DIAGNOSES

❧ Expression Omission Disorder *page 93* ❧
❧ Digit Flotation *page 115* ❧

PART SIX

Aches & Pains
AKA Technique & Movement Problems

> *"These fingers of mine, they got brains in 'em.*
> *You don't tell them what to do – they do it."*
> **Jerry Lee Lewis**

There have been many books, articles, papers and theses written on the subject of piano technique and I'm not about to add another. To attempt to tackle the debates of elbows in or out, or any of the other minutia of how to physically play the piano, is beyond the scope of this book and is not what you came here for. What I will try to give you in this section of *The Piano Practice Physician's Handbook* is help in solving the most common piano technique issues found in piano students.

One of the goals of this book is that you will never

again feel like you are "nagging" your student about the same thing over and over. This has never been truer than in the technique practice section. I hope that you will cease from this point forward to have to say "Curved fingers please!" numerous times in one lesson, and probably several dozen times in one day.

27

Pedal Repulsion
The severe distaste of pedalling

The pedal is, or should be, a pianist's best friend. It can add expression, provides greater harmonic possibilities, and can even disguise errors in one's playing. It really is one of the greatest assets the piano has. Why, then, would some students suffer from *pedal repulsion*?

For many students, I believe it is simply that they have not been taught how to use the pedal effectively or, at the very least, insufficient time has been given in their studies to pedalling instruction. To be confident and comfortable with the pedal, students must understand the mechanics of the pedal, the mechanics of their own feet, and what it is they are trying to achieve with the pedal in each application.

SYMPTOMS

- Reluctance or refusal to use the pedal.
- Poor pedal technique that does not improve upon repetition.
- A belief that one is incapable of pedalling well.

PRESCRIPTIONS

Divide and Conquer

In lesson

To allow for proper processing of pedalling technique, sometimes the best strategy is to remove as many of the other difficulties of piano playing as possible. By putting pedalling in quarantine for a time, we can conquer its challenges before slowly reintroducing it to the rest of piano playing.

In order to isolate the pedalling technique in such a way that can easily be reintegrated later, take one small left hand section from a piece that your student is currently working on, or one that she will be starting soon. A series of a few chords or a slowly moving bassline will work very well. Once you have the left hand snippet chosen, close the book and teach it to your student by rote (or remind her of it if she already knows it).

When she knows this left hand section well you can start to talk about the pedalling. Give her lots of instructions on precisely how it should be pedalled, including even the simplest details that you might think she already knows intuitively. While she is playing instruct her in the timing of the actions, indicating exactly when to release and depress the pedal. If working on legato pedalling you might simply say "foot" to indicate quickly clearing the pedal and "hand" when the next note is to be played. Be as clear as you can and take the time for lots of repetition during the lesson.

At home

Assign practice of this pedalling excerpt alongside your student's regular assignments. Do not ask her to practice anything else with the pedal; the left hand snippet should be her only pedalling assignment. The next week you can choose a new excerpt using the same type of pedalling, further reinforcing the pedalling technique in a new context and still divided from the page.

Continue assigning little chunks of pedalling in this way until you feel the technique has been truly absorbed. Then slowly start to integrate the pedalling back into her regular repertoire. For most students, this will mean pedalling is divided for about a month or so. Take as long as your student needs to really conquer one pedalling technique.

The Naked Piano

In lesson

This is one case where both prescriptions complement each other nicely, and can be used side by side or one after the other, to quickly and comprehensively stop *pedal repulsion* in its tracks. 'The Naked Piano' is the perfect inspirational activity to combine with the isolated practice of 'Divide and Conquer'.

By "naked", I mean of course revealing the strings and actions so that your student can witness the mechanisms of the piano at work. How you go about removing your piano's clothing will depend on your piano. On a grand piano it may be best to set up a mirror so that your student can see inside while she is playing. On an upright piano you will need to remove sections of its casing to reveal the strings. Discuss with your student what the pedal does, how it works, and why we use it. You'll be surprised how much better she will listen to her pedalling when she's also looking at the mechanisms in action.

At home

I don't recommend asking your student to make her own piano at home naked. This could be dangerous if her family doesn't know how, and it's unnecessary. Instead, ask her to draw a picture/diagram of the piano hammers and strings at home and explain to a family member how it all works with the aid of her drawing. Tell her to bring her diagram to the studio to show you, along with the names of family members who now understand piano mechanisms.

RELATED DIAGNOSES

❧ Expression Omission Disorder *page 93* ❧

28
Wrist Drowsiness
The drooping of one's wrists below a sensible height

Low wrists are far from the optimal position for piano playing, as they limit the range of movement available to the pianist. To play piano efficiently the wrist should be roughly level with the keys, depending on the student and the repertoire. This logical argument doesn't stop many young pianists from drooping their wrists down, sometimes enough to rest on the wooden ledge below the keys. These lazy wrists should be cured as soon as possible before the student develops unhealthy finger technique to compensate or sustains a pianistic injury due to the unnecessary strain.

SYMPTOMS

- Wrists positioned below the level of the keys.
- Dropping the wrists unnecessarily.
- Resting the wrists on the ledge below the keys.

PRESCRIPTIONS

River of Doom

In lesson

Tell your student that there is a river running underneath the piano keys, and place your hand at the level of this imaginary river. Ask your student to begin playing her piece, and tell her that if she falls in the 'River of Doom' (touches your hand with her wrist) she'll have to start again. The aim of the game is to get to the end of the piece without falling in once. Persist until this goal is achieved but do take breaks if she is becoming frustrated with the exercise. She may find it very difficult to hold her concentration for this long.

At home

Assign practice with the imaginary 'River of Doom' and tell her you're going to start with the 'River of Doom' first thing next week. Make sure you follow through on this promise and she will learn to practice with the imaginary river to prepare.

Bounce

In lesson

Place a large rubber band or hair elastic around your student's wrist and hold up one end so that the elastic is a little taut. Ask her to push down with her wrist and, while she is doing this, pull up your end gently so that she can only drop it a little before bouncing back up. Allow her to experiment with the different ways she can move her wrist within this setup.

Discuss with her how she can move her wrist up and to the sides as much as she likes, but only 'Bounce' downwards a tiny bit before she springs back up. This is the type of movement she should have at the piano.

Take this elastic wrist setup to the piano. Instruct your student to play her piece/scale (one hand at a time is best) with you still holding the top of the elastic. You won't need to do much to control her wrist movements other than hold it at the right height. Once she has experimented with this in each hand, remove the elastics and ask her to play with the same feeling she had when the elastics were around her wrists. You can prompt her with questions, such as: "Would your wrist be able to go down that far?" or "How did it feel when you did that with the elastic in place?"

At home

Before practicing at home she should do the same elastic exercise, one hand at a time, now holding the upper part of the elastic herself. Tell her to do this before she plays each day and then to try and keep that feeling throughout her practice time. Repeat the full 'Bounce' exercise at the next lesson to reinforce the wrist technique.

RELATED DIAGNOSES

Wrist Lockdown *page 81*
Fused Phalanges *page 118*
Floppy Finger Predicament *page 121*

29

Sticky Tipitis
The tendency of one's fingers to press too firmly into the key

From time to time, you will come across students who seem convinced that the piano keys need to be held down forcefully after they have been played. These students will play the piano keys and then continue to push down on them, sometimes so hard that it appears they want to push all the way through the keybed.

Because of the force that is being exerted into the key currently sounding, students with *sticky tipitis* will often have trouble playing the next key on time or with good articulation. *Sticky tipitis* also creates unnecessary tension and can lead to stresses and strains, so it's important to catch it as early as possible and resolve this tension.

SYMPTOMS

- Fingertips that seem to get stuck at the bottom of each key.
- Slow or reluctant movement from one key to the next.
- Strained, tense fingers when holding a key down.

PRESCRIPTIONS

Sigh It Out

In lesson

Start this exercise with just a five finger pattern or scale. Ask your student to play the scale but to pause after each note to let her hand "sigh". Demonstrate releasing the hand muscles after striking each key.

For this to work it has to be done very slowly, and it may help to ask your student to actually sigh at first to get the feeling of release. Test her sigh by asking her to freeze and wiggling one of her fingers that isn't playing. If she has sighed correctly, you should be able to move her fingers as they will be free of tension. Once she has successfully applied the sighs to her scale, return to her piece and try one hand at a time with the 'Sigh It Out' technique.

At home

Assign practice of all her pieces using the same 'Sigh It Out' technique. When she returns for her next lesson you can start to reduce the sighs, making them shorter and shorter until they eventually become a smooth part of her playing. This process may take several weeks or only one, depending on the level of *sticky tipitis* your student has. Just be patient and continue to practice these hand sighs until the tension fades away.

Soft Landing

In lesson

Close the piano lid or move to a table. Place a cushion, blanket, quilt, teddy or other soft item on the tabletop. Ask your student to play her piece on this padded surface, lifting her arm between notes and landing with the correct finger each time. Encourage her to feel the cushioning effect and how she can rest there between notes.

Return to the piano and ask her to imagine that each piano key has tiny little cushions on its surface. Whenever she plays a key her finger gets to rest on the cushion at the bottom until the note ends. Repeat this full exercise with each piece to develop the imagery and tactile memory of the soft, padded surface.

At home

Encourage your student to practice her pieces in this way all week, using whatever soft items she has at home, before moving to the piano. Ask her to draw soft things at the top of each piece to remind herself to practice 'Soft Landings'. Review the exercise at subsequent lessons as necessary.

RELATED DIAGNOSES

Wrist Lockdown *page 81*
Expression Omission Disorder *page 93*
Fortissimo Fixation *page 96*
Wrist Drowsiness *page 110*
Floppy Finger Predicament *page 121*

ᴗᴗᴗ 30 ᴗᴗᴗ

Digit Flotation

The touching of keys so lightly one's fingers
appear to float on the surface

When students have *digit flotation* there is no weight behind their fingers as they play. Their fingers will appear to float just above the keybed, never fully depressing the key but bouncing away as soon as the note sounds. This leads to (and stems from) awkward, ineffective piano technique.

Much like *pianissimo preoccupation*, I have found this to be more prevalent among adult students and nervous or apprehensive children. It can arise from an effort to not play too loudly, or an uncertainty of the notes they are playing. If not corrected, it not only prevents students from playing loudly and confidently, but from playing with a true, smooth legato as well. This is because it is not possible to transfer weight between fingers if there is no weight behind the finger to begin with.

Symptoms

- Not using arm weight to play the keys.
- Very soft or tentative playing.
- Failure to fully depress each key down to the keybed.
- Frequent notes which do not fully sound.

Prescriptions

Grasshopper

In lesson

If your student is currently using legato, this activity will require a little hiatus from that for a while. You will return to legato of course, but it's quite important that she removes it completely from her playing for the time being. Transitioning to a new way of playing will be hard, especially if your student has been learning for a while, and she will need to let go of the old technique completely to be successful.

Place your hand and your student's hand in any five-finger position, such as the C pentascale. Play a simple pattern and ask her to echo it back to you exactly as you played it. Play with a non-legato (portato) touch and hop completely off the keys between each note. Your fingers (and your student's fingers) should leave the piano entirely between notes, even though you are not changing positions. Use the analogy of a grasshopper hopping between blades of grass to make this clearer and more memorable. Repeat the copycatting several times with each hand, watching her hands carefully as she plays.

Once you feel she is comfortable with this new way of playing, and she is landing with her full arm weight on each key, apply this same touch to all her assignments. Go through everything she will be practicing this week together and have her play each piece, scale or exercise with the 'Grasshopper' technique.

At home

Assign 'Grasshopper' practice for all of your student's current assignments. Ask her to draw grasshoppers at the top of each page so she will remember to play this way at home. It will most likely take several weeks of practicing this way for her to feel really comfortable lifting and falling into each key.

When you feel she has truly conquered this new way of playing, reintroduce some legato playing. Proceed cautiously at first, perhaps only choosing one piece to play legato and keeping all other assignments in 'Grasshopper' mode for another several weeks. In time, she will become less and less reliant on the 'Grasshopper' technique to find her arm weight.

Magnetic Attraction

In lesson

This remedy is almost exactly the opposite of the 'Grasshopper' prescription above. Both will be effective for different students and in different situations. Occasionally, both might be needed to truly cure the problem of *digit flotation*. If you're unsure which one to choose, start with 'Magnetic Attraction' for milder cases, and 'Grasshopper' for more severe cases.

Ask your student to close her eyes for a moment and hold up her hands. Tell her that you are attaching invisible magnets to each of her fingertips. The matching magnets are underneath the keys, right at the bottom. Since they're so far away from each other right now, the magnetic attraction isn't working yet, but the closer they get to each other the more they will be pulled together. The magnets will start to activate once she begins to depress a key down, pulling her finger right to the bottom of the key and holding it there for the length of the note.

Once you have finished this description, ask her to open her eyes again. She should now play her piece, very slowly, imagining the magnets activating as she plays. Reinforce the story and encourage her to feel the magnetic pull down to the bottom of the key as she plays.

At home

At the end of the lesson tell your student that you're going to loan your magic piano magnets to her this week

– mime taking them off each of her fingers and placing them in her piano bag for safekeeping.

Tell her she needs to put the magnets on each day before she starts her practice and write a note on her music or in her notebook/binder so she doesn't forget. You can gradually wean her off the magnet story as time goes on and her technique improves, but you will always have that strong visual to refer back to if the problem re-emerges.

RELATED DIAGNOSES

❧ Articulation Anaemia *page 73* ☙
❧ Expression Omission Disorder *page 93* ☙
❧ Pianissimo Preoccupation *page 99* ☙
❧ Wrist Drowsiness *page 110* ☙

31

Fused Phalanges
The apparent inability to bend one's finger joints

Students with *fused phalanges* have been making piano teachers groan, fret and sigh for a long time. Those straight fingers are far from the optimal hand shape for piano students, and cause many related problems along the way, such as uneven scale passages, poor tone production and jerky legato.

The difficulty has always been that no matter how much we remind, nag and plead with students to curve their fingers during the lesson, it doesn't always carry through to their home practice. The quandary is how to make it become an ingrained, instinctive habit.

The prescriptions below are more appealing and memorable than a verbal reminder and, therefore, more likely to be practiced. But you will still have to be persistent – it takes many iterations to make something a habit.

Symptoms

- Long, straight fingers when playing the piano.
- Thumbs that do not comfortably reach the keys.
- Playing the keys with a large portion of the finger, instead of just the pad of the finger.

Prescriptions

Spider Safety

In lesson

This solution is not recommended for students who hate spiders; in that case you may want to pick a different creature to protect.

Close the piano lid and ask your student to make her best piano hand shape on the surface of the lid. Help to form a good round hand shape with the bridge of her hand lifted, explaining that a little spider needs to live underneath her hand. It climbs under there for safety and if she lets her hand fall the spider won't have a home. Part of our job when playing the piano is to look after this little spider.

Open the lid up again and ask her to place her hands on the keys, ready to begin playing. She can begin playing her piece, but she needs to keep her spider house up. If it collapses she must start from the beginning again. If your student's piece is on the longer side, do this exercise section by section so that the beginning of the piece doesn't get over-practiced.

At home

Review the 'Spider Safety' technique at the end of the lesson. Assign practice with the spider's house in place throughout. Ask your student to also practice making her spider house when she is away from the piano, for example, in the car, waiting for a bus, or any other opportunity she gets. The more practice she has in making this shape, the stronger and safer her spider's house will become.

X Marks the Spot

In lesson

When you use 'X Marks the Spot' you won't have to continue to nag about hand shape. You won't even have to mention it at all. By taking the focus away from the shape of the hand you allow your student to get a new perspective on why we insist on this hand position, and perhaps come to "discover" the correct hand shape for herself.

Get some sticky tabs, notes or repositionable stickers (make sure they are cleanly removable without leaving a mark). If you don't have sticky notes or stickers that are suitable, this activity is still possible – your imaginations will just have to work a little harder! Cut the sticky tabs down so that they are about 2.5 cm (1 in) squared (you can draw little Xs on each one if you really want to sell the 'X Marks the Spot' theme). Stick these to the keys your student needs to use in the piece she is working on, positioning them about halfway between the edges of the keys and the black keys in the "sweet spot". If there are black keys used in the piece place those stickers just a little in from the edge of the black key, as shown in the diagram.

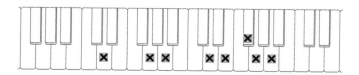

Ask your student to play her piece, trying to hit as many of these targets as she can, and aiming to keep her fingers roughly over the targets when they're not playing. She may figure out for herself after a few repetitions that to do this she will have to curve her fingers.

If she doesn't catch on to the optimal finger position for 'X Marks the Spot' have a discussion about how she could make all her fingers sit above the targets, and what her hand might look like. It's best if she does some of the work to realise this herself, so don't be too hasty to intervene and explain.

At home

Stick the "target spots" directly onto her sheet music and show her how to position them on her keys at home. You might want to make a diagram or involve a parent to help her position them correctly. Continue applying this technique in the lesson and at home and eventually you will be able to graduate to imaginary target spots.

RELATED DIAGNOSES

❧ Fortissimo Fixation *page 96* ❧
❧ Wrist Drowsiness *page 110* ❧
❧ Floppy Finger Predicament *page 121* ❧

32

Floppy Finger Predicament
The collapsing of the top finger joint when pressing a key

This is not to be confused with *fused phalanges*. If students have *floppy finger predicament*, their hand shape will be curved but their finger joints will bend backward as they play the keys. This is extremely common in young students and even more so in students with long, slender fingers.

It is imperative that this is resolved as soon as possible on the piano journey and preferably before the student begins to use legato. It takes a lot of determination on the part of the student, teacher and parent to persist and develop the technique needed to create firm fingertips out of floppy ones. The prescriptions below will help ease this process, but you should still be prepared to be vigilant for quite some time.

SYMPTOMS

- A backward bend in the finger when a key is pressed down.
- Playing the key with the full top section of the finger.
- An inability to keep a round hand shape due to collapsing fingers.

PRESCRIPTIONS

The Bionic Pianist

In lesson

This solution will help your student to move her whole arm as one unit, thus avoiding pushing into each finger. If you suspect that the reason your student's finger joints are collapsing is because she is pushing unnecessarily into the key, this is a great way to change the way she moves and thinks about her arms and hands at the piano.

Give your student a pencil, preferably with an eraser on the end. Ask her to hold the pencil in her hand, eraser side down. This is her new "bionic hand". Tell her to play her piece using her bionic hand and encourage her to move her whole arm up and down to play each key. She shouldn't lock her wrist but it should be kept in a reasonably stable position making a straight line from her elbow to her knuckles.

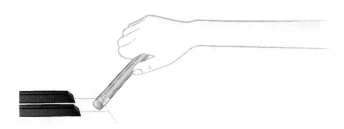

Have her use the bionic hand to play one hand at a time first, and then hands together. After several repetitions using the bionic pencil hands, tell her she's going to try a new type of bionic hand now.

Help her make a closed hand shape with her thumb behind her second finger, supporting the joint (sometimes called a "braced finger" in piano method books). Instruct her to play her piece with this new bionic hand, keeping the same motion in her arms that she needed to play with the pencils. Repeat this several times, changing around the finger she supports with her thumb.

After she has tried out each finger in a bionic hand shape, she can open her hands out once more to play. Ask her to play her piece with regular fingering now, but imagining that a thumb is strengthening each finger, or that her fingers are as firm as a pencil. Don't rush her to play legato with her bionic hands but, if she does try it herself and manages to keep her fingertips firm, don't discourage her either.

At home

Assign practice of each of these stages, reducing the number of steps according to the amount of time your student has to practice each day. For example, if she has time for three repetitions she should do the first with bionic pencil hands, the second with bionic braced fingers (she can choose which finger) and the third with an open hand shape. Continue to assign this type of practice until the *floppy finger predicament* is cured, and reassign if it returns at any stage.

Tap Drills

In lesson

Isolating the action required to play the piano from the actual piano keys can really help students who are struggling to control that pesky top finger joint. You will have to be very persistent with this technique, and it's best if the parents are helping out at home too. Over time, though, the condition should improve and you will be able to rely on your student's firm fingertips.

Close the piano lid or move to a table and place your student's music in front of both of you. Hold your right hand over the hard surface and demonstrate by tapping down with your fingertip in a nice curved shape. Ask your student to copy you, and try out each finger. Correct her action as needed, explaining which part of the finger she should be tapping with and the right technique to use.

After warming up in this way with each hand, tap

out your student's piece together. Tap the right hand first, then the left, and then hands together, all the time watching her hands for any collapsing fingers or odd techniques.

Once the 'Tap Drills' are completed, return to the keys and tell her to keep the same firm feeling in her fingertips that she had while tapping it out. If a finger does fall down, pause the playing and ask her to tap that finger on the fallboard or bench to "test" it, and then restart from that spot. Repeat the 'Tap Drills' before each and every piece.

At home

Assign 'Tap Drills' for each piece during the week and ask a parent to help with reminders if possible. You may need to assign fewer pieces due to the extra time it will take your student to practice each one, but it will be worth it if you can fix her *floppy finger predicament*. It's important that you follow through with this in the next lesson and continue to expect the 'Tap Drills' before each piece. Over time, your student will carry the process over to her home practice if she forms the habit during the lesson.

Related Diagnoses

Fortissimo Fixation *page 96*
Wrist Drowsiness *page 110*
Sticky Tipitis *page 112*
Fused Phalanges *page 118*

Forging Your Own Path and Discovering New Cures

Assuming you've read through *The Piano Practice Physician's Handbook* and not skipped right to the end, you now have the 32 piano practice ailments and their prescriptions fresh in your mind. So what are you going to do with this information? What is your next step?

I hope it is not to tuck this book away on a bookshelf somewhere to gather dust for years to come. Instead, I hope you will place this handbook within reach of your desk so you can return to it again and again. Not all the ailments will be immediately relevant to the students you have right now, but that doesn't mean they won't be relevant in the future.

The next time you encounter a student who just will not play on her fingertips, who speeds up her recital piece, or who consistently plays in the incorrect octave, don't pull out your hair or throw up your hands in desperation. Come back instead to these pages and find solace in a practice prescription. I have never found a practice issue that didn't have a workable creative solution once I pinpointed the heart of the issue.

If you can't find your student's ailment in this little handbook, I hope you will not give up there. Being a great piano practice physician means you sometimes need to go off-map. Forge your own path through the thickets of practice maladies, diagnosing and treating as you go. And if you do discover an intriguing remedy, let other teachers in on your secret. Practice physicians are a generous and helpful breed after all.

I'll leave you here. My parting wish is that you will continue to see yourself as an inquisitive and analytical piano practice physician, diagnosing and treating the ailments of your piano students as they arise. I promise your piano studio will be a more productive, rewarding and enjoyable place if you do.

Acknowledgements

My sincerest thanks to my wonderful, patient and diligent proofreader Janine Levine. Without her assistance these pages would have been filled with the garbled ramblings of a piano teacher instead of the thoughtful and clear advice that I hope you have found.

Writing a book in the language of music and movement is no easy task and I had many choices to consider and deliberate over in order to make the book as clear, useful and practical as possible. Janine's assistance with the art of writing was invaluable and has made this book what it is. Furthermore, she balanced her keen attention to detail with an encouraging warmth and kindness, and made the editing process delightfully pain-free, even enjoyable.

Thanks also to the many excellent and lovely teachers who I connect with online on a daily basis. These teachers from around the world challenge, inspire and push me to become a better educator. Finding these communities of piano teachers has provided me not only with ideas, information and insight but also with an even greater love of music and the craft of teaching.

I am so grateful to live in a time when the closed, secretive doors of music studios are being gleefully flung open. Teachers all over the globe are realising that there is more to be gained from giving information freely than keeping it close to one's chest. I believe that this generous, unrestricted sharing of ideas is what will continue to move music education forward for many generations to come.

Ailment Index

LEAP PHOBIA   14
The habitual slowing of one's tempo to prepare for a leap

LINE LIMP   65
The belief that barlines are signs for one to stop or yield

NOTE DEAFNESS   91
The inability to hear incorrect notes played by oneself

OBSTACLE SNEEZES   59
The propensity to pause before playing a difficult section

OCTAVE DISORIENTATION   17
The confounding of notes with the same name in different octaves

More from Nicola Cantan

Thank you for reading *The Piano Practice Physician's Handbook*. If you liked it please leave a review wherever you purchased the book, and take a look at the further resources below.

Colourful Keys Blog

Nicola writes regular articles and shares ideas on her blog at: *www.colourfulkeys.ie/blog*. Check it out if you're looking for more piano teaching inspiration.

Piano Physician Bonuses

Download the printables mentioned in this book at: *www.pianophysician.com/bonus*. These resources will make it quick and easy for you to assign the prescriptions and help your student to follow through at home.

The Piano Physician's Clinic Course

There is an accompanying course to this handbook for those teachers looking to go into more depth with the practice ailments and prescriptions. This video course will take you through each and every practice ailment, what causes it and how to implement the proper cure. There is also an exclusive community as part of this the *Piano Physician's Clinic* course where you can get help and advice about your students' practice issues.

To get more information and preview the course go to: *www.pianophysician.com/course*. Use the coupon code "HANDBOOK2017" to get $10 off if you choose to buy.

74392753R00084

Made in the USA
San Bernardino, CA
16 April 2018